USIN
CONSULTANT

Achieving results,
adding value

Michael Armstrong graduated from the London School of Economics, and is a Fellow of the Institute of Personnel Management and a Fellow of the Institute of Management Consultants. He spent 12 years in general personnel management in the food and engineering industries followed by 10 years as a management consultant with Coopers & Lybrand, where he headed up the personnel consultancy division. From 1976 to 1988 he was Personnel Director of Book Club Associates and since then he has practised as an independent HR consultant. His books include *Personnel and the Bottom Line, Management Processes and Functions* and, with Helen Murlis, *Reward Management.*

USING THE HR CONSULTANT

*Achieving results,
adding value*

Michael Armstrong

INSTITUTE OF PERSONNEL MANAGEMENT

First published in 1994

Phototypeset in Times by
The Comp-Room, Aylesbury
and printed in Great Britain by
The Cromwell Press, Melksham

British Library Cataloguing in Publication Data

Armstrong, Michael
    Using the HR Consultant: Achieving
    Results, Adding Value. – (Developing
    Skills Series)
    I. Title   II. Series
    658.3

ISBN 0-85292-546-8

INSTITUTE OF PERSONNEL MANAGEMENT
IPM House, Camp Road, Wimbledon, London SW19 4UX
Tel: 081-946-9100   Fax: 081-947-2570
Registered office as above. Registered Charity No. 215797
A company limited by guarantee. Registered in England No. 198002

Contents

Introduction

HR consultancy – a growth business

More use is being made of management consultants to advise on human resource (HR) issues today than ever before. The reasons for this are fairly obvious. While HR departments are being slimmed down, especially in the centre of large organisations, the need to innovate and manage change is becoming ever more important to ensure that organisations survive and thrive in a highly competitive world. Consultants are therefore frequently used as catalysts or change agents.

The pressure to innovate may come from top managers who have discovered human resource management (HRM), read a few articles (even a book), attended a conference or two, and are now seeking the holy grail which will transform their organisation – its performance, productivity, capacity for renewal and growth, ability to increase shareholder value and deliver value to customers, and so on. They may well have simplistic views about the power of such panaceas as peformance-related pay, performance management and competency profiling.

HR professionals may therefore find themselves in the position of following their leaders and having to work with consultants to turn their leaders' vision into reality. But it has been known for HR directors and managers to be equally guilty of thinking, in effect, 'it's new so let's use it' and then saying they need outside independent help. Those who pursue the latest fads are major contributors to the growth of HR consultancy. Richard Pascale[1] has illustrated effectively how fads have come (with a flourish of trumpets) and gone (like thieves in the night) over the years.

The number of HR consultancies and consultants has risen in response to these new demands (And also, it must be said, to create some of them). In the 1960s there were remarkably few general personnel consultants such as PA and Urwick Orr. The large accountancy firms such as Coopers & Lybrand, Price Waterhouse and KPMG Peat Marwick (as it now is), who are now major players in the HR field, had hardly started to move into this area. Coopers & Lybrand appointed its first personnel consultant (myself) in 1966. There were, of course, also a number of more specialised consultancies in the pay, work-study and training fields, such as Hay and the Ann Shaw Organisation, and there were also the recruitment consultants who began to emerge as a major force in the 1960s.

Since then HR consultancies and consultants have proliferated. The large general firms have expanded and many smaller specialised firms (the 'boutiques') have been set up. This growth was accelerated not only by the factors mentioned above but also by the 'training revolution' of the 1970s, the behavioural science movement of the same decade (organisation development, job enrichment and the like) and the greatly increased interest in reward management in the 1980s, especially in the areas of performance-related pay, performance management and flexible benefits.

The last decade has also seen a massive growth in the number of independent HR consultants, partly because many victims of the recession have turned to consultancy, some of them hoping that it will be an easy option (it is not). Academics, especially from the burgeoning business schools and the former polytechnics, have joined the throng.

There is no way of estimating how many HR consultants there are. Anyone can become a consultant and there is no national register, only the register of HR consultants held by the Institute of Personnel Management and the one held for its members by the only professional consultancy association, the Institute of Management Consultants. However, it is safe to assume that there are several thousand; many are excellent and highly experienced, some are not so good and relatively inexperienced, and there are some cowboys around whose only mission is to sell their simplistic prescriptions to any or all of the problems which beset managements.

It is also worth noting that structural changes in organisations have led to changes in the roles of HR specialists, many of whom are becoming internal consultants. One of the issues which will be discussed in this book (in Chapter 12) is how this internal consultancy role can operate as an alternative to or in association with external consultants.

This pressure for the use of consultants and the often bewildering choice available to those who want to engage them, can make it difficult to ensure the success of a consultancy assignment.

One of the recurring themes of this book will be that the onus for achieving the required results must always be on the sponsor of the project, and the rest of the book will describe the approaches which HR specialists can use to achieve success and obtain added value from the consultants they engage.

Why are HR consultants engaged?

HR consultants are engaged for two main reasons: first, to get results by innovating new systems and procedures and by helping to solve problems; and secondly, to add value to the people management processes within organisations through the use of their experience and expertise.

Good consultants, well managed by their clients, will provide value for money. This has certainly been my experience as an HR director or manager at the receiving end of consultancy advice. On the odd occasions when things go seriously wrong, it is often because the *clients* have commissioned the wrong study, picked the wrong consultant, failed to clarify the objectives and deliverables of the assignment, neglected to monitor the assignment carefully enough or not taken sufficient care over the implementation and change management processes.

Of course consultancy assignments can go wrong in a number of ways: deadlines are not met, the terms of reference are not fulfilled, the advice is unacceptable, the implementation goes wrong and so on. But the message of this book is that problems are avoidable by adopting the following approach.

1. Take care to ensure that you have a valid reason for using consultants – that the study is worth doing and could not be done equally well or better internally.
2. Specify the objectives and deliverables of the assignment in a way which clearly indicates that the desired results are worthwhile and achievable.
3. Source and 'select the consultants with great care. Always consider alternatives even if you already have someone in mind. Approach reputable firms and individuals. Give preference to individuals who are members of professional institutions: the Institute of Personnel Management, the Institute of

Training and Development or the Institute of Management Consultants. Always take up references if you do not know them. Always meet and approve the actual consultants who will carry out the job.
4. Plan the project meticulously with the consultants. Agree terms of reference, deadlines, deliverables, methods of monitoring and reviewing projects and reporting arrangements. Ensure that both you and the consultants fully understand your respective roles in the assignment.
5. Manage the project. You are purchasing someone else's services, so it is up to you to ensure that they deliver.
6. Bear in mind, however, that the best consultancy projects are those in which the client and the consultant work in partnership.
7. Remember that all consultancy projects involve change. Take particular care therefore over the implementation, involvement and communication processes during *and* after the assignment.

Organisation of the book

This book starts with an analysis of the role of consultants and how they interact with their clients. It then addresses the question: 'Why use consultants?' The major areas in which HR/personnel consultants are engaged and the ways they operate are then briefly described before I tackle the sequential areas of activity required to make the best use of HR consultants: establishing the need, sourcing consultants, starting and managing assignments, and implementing recommendations. The use of internal consultants is then considered and the book concludes with a chapter on getting it right, which, with the help of case studies, examines the things that *can* go wrong with a consultancy assignment – not something which happens frequently, I am glad to say, but when it does it is painful. More positively, this chapter summarises what should be done to ensure that things go right.

Throughout the book, the term HR consultant is used as being synonymous with personnel consultant.

1
The Role of the
Management Consultant

HR consultants are specialists within the general field of management consultancy. What follows is a description of the role of management consultants in general, but it applies to the work of all types of consultants, including those concerned mainly with HR matters; whatever their specialism, consultants generally apply their experience in the same way, and use a similar range of skills.

What management consultants do

As defined by the Institute of Management Consultants, a management consultant is an independent and qualified person who provides a professional service to business, public and other undertakings by:

- identifying and investigating problems concerned with strategy, policy, markets, organisation, procedures and methods;
- formulating recommendations for appropriate action by factual investigation and analysis with due regard for broader management and business implications;
- discussing and agreeing with the client the most appropriate course of action;
- providing assistance where required by the client to implement recommendations.

In carrying out these activities, professional management consultants should be expected to exercise independence of thought and action, deal with management problems in perspective, give well-balanced advice and continuously strive to improve their professional skills and to maintain a high quality of service.

Management consultants have a number of different but often

1

closely linked roles. They may be problem solvers who are presented with a deteriorating situation or an issue and asked to produce recommendations on how it should be dealt with. They may play an innovatory role, developing new structures, systems and procedures on behalf of their clients or advising on 'process change' – how things are done as well as what is done. Consultants may simply function as 'an extra pair of hands', doing things which people within the organisation are perfectly capable of doing but which they do not have the time or the inclination to do. They may sometimes be used to gather facts, as in a benchmarking exercise to analyse best practice in comparable organisations.

More generally, consultants can be brought in, either by the organisation itself or by some other body, to carry out an audit – a health check. This may be a general review of the effectiveness of current policies and practices or it may be a much more fundamental and rigorous scrutiny of the organisation's basic functions and processes. Business process re-engineering studies come into this category.

Sometimes, consultants are engaged to carry out an investigation or review of a matter which is too delicate or controversial to be conducted by someone within the organisation. This review may be commissioned by an external body or group of individuals (for example non-executive directors) who are concerned about how the organisation is being run and want a confidential and independent report on the state of affairs and what needs to be done about it. Such reviews are often about fundamental aspects of performance, organisation or financial management and may include a rigorous study of organisational efficiency and the scope for cutting costs, including employment costs. They may not be directly concerned with HR issues but they will almost always have implications for human resource management. Frequently, the head of HR is not involved at all in commissioning such studies and in some cases may only play an incidental or peripheral part in the investigation and in the discussion of findings and recommendations. The role of the HR director in such circumstances is discussed in Chapter 10.

Finally, and importantly, management consultants can act as change agents – identifying and developing levers for change and helping to implement and manage the change process. In this role they are facilitators who are deploying their independent point of view and their expertise in process consulting and change management in order to achieve the smooth and acceptable introduction of change. This is an overarching role which affects all the other consultancy roles.

How they do it

How management consultants operate will, of course, vary enormously, depending on the type of organisation, their remit and their own preferences and skills. Their approaches will also vary according to the main areas in which they are working. These are:

- *strategic studies* – the development of broad strategies and policies and major revisions to organisational structures and activities to meet long-term requirements;
- *systems development* – the introduction or amendment of systems and procedures;
- *problem solving* – providing solutions to organisational and management problems;
- *service provision* – the delivery of services such as recruitment, selection and training which could be carried out within the organisation;
- *process consulting* – the provision of advice and help in process areas such as organisation, planning, objective setting, quality management, performance management, team building, conflict resolution and, importantly, change management.

Key consultancy activities

There is no such thing as a typical assignment, but some or all of the consultancy activities described below are likely to take place in most assignments.

Identification Initially, the consultant discusses with the client the reasons for the assignment, its objectives and the terms of reference, if necessary conducting a special survey to collect the relevant facts. Clients will start with their own definitions,

3

but it is the duty of the consultant to question and test these definitions to ensure that they have been thought through and to obtain essential data on the background to the assignment and the environment in which it is to take place. Consultants must attempt at this point to establish whether or not there is any 'hidden agenda'. The reasons given for calling them in are not always the real ones, and these underlying factors may not be articulated by clients, indeed, may not even be understood by them. An experienced consultant will always want answers at this stage to such questions as: 'Who *really* wants the assignment to take place and why?' 'To what exent is it likely to be supported – or opposed – by top management, middle management, the workforce in general and, if relevant, the trade unions?' 'What resources – money, time, people – is the organisation prepared to invest in it?'

Project planning This involves decisions on what work needs to be done, who does it, the timetable, the costs involved and methods of monitoring and controlling progress. Management consultants normally set out their views on these matters in their proposal but these preliminary assessments have to be developed into much more detailed project schedules which specify the 'deliverables' at each stage, especially in larger and more complex assignments.

Data collection The first stage in any assignment is the collection of data about the organisation itself (as a whole, or only the part in which the consultant is operating), the environment in which it exists, the situation facing it, the present arrangements, and the views of those concerned.

The information on present arrangements will include fairly specific data on strategies, policies, structures, systems, procedures and work flows. It may, and in most cases should, also cover process issues relating to the culture of the organisation (its norms and values), its climate, its management style, how people interact, and generally 'the way things are done around here'.

The data may be collected by sifting documents, by interviews, meetings and observation, or by conducting special attitude or opinion surveys.

Analysis   In the analysis stage, what may be a complex mass of data is subjected to close and systematic examination so that it can be resolved into its key elements. This process of identification and dissection aims to facilitate the orderly arrangement of the data (which may be present in a confused state) into logical patterns, thus promoting understanding and pointing the way to an appropriate diagnosis and decision.

Analysis concentrates on facts but will also subject opinions to critical examination to establish the extent to which they are founded on fact. The aim of the analysis will be to provide a precise structure and terminology for the assignment which will serve as a means of communication and enable those involved to make their judgements within a clearly defined framework.

Diagnosis   This is the process of identifying the root cause or causes of the problem (not the symptoms) or the real needs of the organisation in the area under review. A good diagnosis will be based on rigorous analysis and will establish not only the immediate factors to be taken into account but the longer-term causes or implications. As far as possible the diagnosis will be specific, but it might be necessary to present a general picture of the context in which the situation has arisen which has prompted the need for action. The diagnosis should certainly avoid simplistic explanations.

Recommendations   These should flow logically from the analysis and diagnosis. There will inevitably be alternative solutions or courses of action which will have to be evaluated. Good consultants will always formulate their recommendations in conjunction with their clients. This will involve testing the alternatives, and this is often an iterative process as, through further analysis and discussion, the way forward becomes clearer.

The recommendations should indicate how they should be implemented and the timetable and costs of implementation.

Feedback   Although the consultant's recommendations will probably have been formulated jointly with the client, it is still necessary for them to be fed back to any individuals directly concerned with the assignment and to project teams or steering groups. It may also be necessary for the consultant to advise on and take part in the communication and consultation process with employees and their representatives. The feedback to the sponsors of the assignment may take the shape of a formal document, but the old days of voluminous consultants' reports have now largely gone. Many consultants present their findings as 'bullet points' in a highly readable form which is amplified by oral presentations, with supporting data made available as necessary.

This approach reflects a move away from the old concept of management consultants as people with all the answers who delivered their pronouncements, as it were, on tablets of stone, and then left their clients to get on with it (or not, as was frequently the case).

Agreement The agreement to go ahead with the recommendations, in whole, in part or as amended following discussion, should lead to the preparation of an implentation programme which will specify how, if at all, the consultant will help.

Implementation Two totally contradictory remarks are often made about consultants: first that 'once you've got them you can't get rid of them', and secondly that 'they are only too anxious to rush off to a new assignment leaving their client to clear up the mess'. In fact, good consultants will want to help with implementation, not because it provides extra fee income (although that may be a consideration) but because they genuinely believe they have a role as change agents in assisting in the process of converting ideas into action. They are not there just to be prescriptive. Such consultants relish the challenge of getting people to understand, accept and act on their recommendations, and welcome the opportunity to become involved in the change management processes. So although some consultants are indeed butterflies, flitting from flower to flower, the majority derive their job satisfaction from being involved in the process of ensuring that the recommendations to which they have contributed really work.

Follow-up and evaluation Consultants may be asked to follow up the assignment to evaluate its impact and make suggestions on any amendments to the original recommendations which experience has shown to be necessary.

Consultancy skills and behaviours

Management consultants use their subject expertise, developed by education, training and, largely, experience, on behalf of their clients. Ultimately, however, it is the skill with which that expertise is used which differentiates the good from the not-so-good consultant.

Consultancy skills are essentially those required to carry out the various activities referred to above. They include analytical ability, diagnostic and interactive skills and the ability to communicate clearly and persuasively. Clearly the mix of skills will vary in different types of assignments. Analytical and diagnostic skills will be particularly important in problem solving. Interactive and oral skills will be critical in training or selection. Process consultants (those advising on such processes as organisation, team building and continuous development) will require a wide range of skills to carry out the various roles they play as facilitators of change, ranging from listening and observing to stimulating action. Even consultants not specialising in process issues will need a variety of skills, because consultancy interventions always involve process considerations.

Schmidt and Johnson[2] have suggested that there is a continuum of behaviour used by consultants from the relatively passive to the highly active, as follows:

1. *Listening.* Effective consultants *listen* to their clients. As facilitators their role may be to uncover and release the good ideas that may already exist in profusion around the organisation. Sometimes it might seem regrettable that an outsider has to be engaged to unlock these ideas, but one of the most important roles a consultant can play is that of a catalyst – stimulating ideas and change. Consultants can not only help to release ideas but can also analyse, assess and structure them so that they combine to make a powerful contribution to the achievement of change. Consultants listen, and then engage in the reflecting, clarifying, interpreting and probing behaviours described below before feeding back the outcomes to their clients. This lays them open to Peter Townsend's well-known gibe about consultants:[3] 'They borrow your watch to tell the time and then steal it.' But this

7

process of listening to and releasing ideas is one of the most useful contributions a consultant can make.

2. *Reflecting*. This is what consultants do when they mirror the client's ideas so that they can be expressed more freshly and objectively.

3. *Clarifying*. One step further from reflecting, consultants rephrase their client's statements so that they become clearer, sharper and more precise.

4. *Interpreting*. The next step is for the consultant to express what the client is trying to say, often in different but clearer terms. Interpretation may require putting together the implications of several statements.

5. *Probing*. Here consultations elicit from their clients ideas and opinions which the latter may not have expressed or even be fully aware of.

6. *Providing new data*. The consultant provides new ideas or information from their own experience which will enlarge the horizons of the client and open the way to new approaches which may not previously have been considered.

7. *Identifying options for action*. Consultants help their clients to expand the range of possible actions in the light of the previous analysis. This is the stage where synergy should take place between the ideas and experience of the client and those of the consultant.

8. *Proposing criteria for evaluation of alternatives*. Their client will be helped to select the best course of action by suggesting criteria to use in evaluation and helping to arrange the possible choices in order of preference.

9. *Recommending*. At this stage the consultant advises the client on which of the potential actions is best, having ensured that the client is aware of all the options. The recommendation may be mild or forceful, and it will be supported by reasons. Good consultants, however, will remember that their clients must make the decision, because it is the client, not the consultant, who has to live with the consequences.

10. *Prescribing*. This is the extreme form of recommending in which consultants use the weight of their authority and expertise to tell their clients what they must do.

11. *Planning the implementation*. This is the ultimate use of the experience of consultants in which they not only prescribe

what should be done but also develop the detailed stages for doing it.

An appreciation of the roles of consultants, the skills they have to use and the problems they may have to face is a necessary start to the process of getting the best results from an assignment. It will help to ensure that the consultants make an added value contribution in the various areas in which they can be used, as described in the next chapter.

2

Areas of Human Resource Management Consultancy

Human resource management consultancy assignments can take place in any area of HR management. They can take the form of strategy, policy, systems or process innovation and development, problem solving, or the provision of specialist services. The main areas can be categorised as follows:

- general advice on HR issues;
- the analysis and diagnosis of HR problems and advice on their solution;
- systems development and problem solving;
- process development and problem solving;
- training services delivery;
- recruitment and selection services delivery;
- benchmarking.

General advice

General advice on HR issues can deal with strategies, policies, procedures or practices.

HR strategies cover decisions on what developments should take place in the longer term in HR policies, processes, procedures and practices. This is the broadest area of HR consultancy. It is also probably the one in which the least use is made of outside advice, since strategic considerations are very much the affair of top management, who may well feel that outsiders have nothing to contribute.

HR policies cover such areas as employment, pay, training and development, equal opportunities, health and safety, employee relations, joint consultation and communications.

HR procedures define the required modes of dealing with employment matters such as discipline, grievance handling, redundancy, appointments, promotion, transfers, job grading and

10

health and safety audits. They are often governed, or at least influenced, by employment, equal opportunity, equal pay, race relations and health and safety legislation. The definition, implementation and review of such procedures should be well within the capability of any HR professional and outside help in writing them is seldom required when such a person is employed in the organisation. However, smaller organisations or those just starting out, which may not have an HR function, may gain from the advice of consultants in developing a basic set of procedures, if only to ensure that they do not get involved in messy and expensive industrial tribunal cases.

HR practices consist of all the routine administrative tasks carried out by HR departments: recruitment, induction training, maintaining manual records, administering pay and (if they still exist) merit rating systems, arranging transfers and dealing with individual employees on such matters as maternity leave, personal problems and problems related to their work. It is most unlikely that management consultants will become involved in these routines unless their advice is sought on setting up an HR function.

HR problems

Outside consultants are sometimes asked to use their expertise and/or their independent judgement to help solve fundamental HR problems affecting the organisation as a whole. These problems might take the form of high rates of employee turnover or low morale, poor productivity or levels of performance, skills shortages, an inadequate supply of potential senior managers, an unsatisfactory climate of industrial relations, a fundamental lack of trust between management and employees, interdepartmental conflicts, poor teamwork or an ineffective organisational structure. There is never a shortage of HR problems in most organisations.

Consultants can help with all these types of problems, although before calling them in to deal with more serious matters the question has to be asked: 'However expert and independent they may be, will they really be able to get to the fundamental issues, which are probably buried in our particular culture and traditions and which outsiders will not be able to understand because they can never get close enough to them?'

The answer to this question may be that the objectivity, analytical skills and experience of good consultants equip them to get at the root of the problems, a process which is much more difficult for people who have been living with them for some time. Consultants can also trade on their independence to use attitude surveys and focus group meetings (discussions with selected groups of employees which concentrate on a number of key issues) to elicit the true opinions and feelings of employees about the organisation and how it treats them.

But there is no easy answer. Some organisations only call for outside help when the problem has become intractable, when political factions within the company make it impossible to reach a consensus or when the problem is so sensitive that only outsiders can be used to solve it. In these circumstances a consultant can cut through the undergrowth and, using process consulting techniques, bring the factions together to seek a generally acceptable solution.

Systems development

Systems development assignments are concerned with the introduction or improvement of systems or processes for HR planning, job evaluation, reward management (pay structures and pay-for-performance schemes), employee benefits, performance management, human resource development and computerised personnel records.

The use of the term 'system' can, however, be misleading in many areas of HR management. A system can be defined as something consisting of a connected set of parts which, in the field of management, involves considered principles of procedure. It implies something that will operate to a predetermined pattern in accordance with given principles, laws or mechanisms. To refer, for example, to performance management as a system implies that it is only necessary to pull various levers (setting objectives and measuring, rating and reviewing performance) and various desirable outcomes in the shape of improved performance will be the inevitable result. But it is not like that at all.

Performance management is much more a process of interaction between two people consisting of dialogues and agreements which define what can be expected to be achieved, what constitutes good performance and how improved levels of performance can be attained. These discussions do indeed take place within a framework which could be described as a system, but what counts is *how* the various activities contained in the framework are carried out, not the framework itself. The same point applies to other 'systems' such as job evaluation, pay structures, performance-related pay and HR development.

This is why, although process development in such fields as leadership, interpersonal skills and teamworking is treated here as a separate category of HR consulting, most if not all systems assignments must include a considerable element of process consulting if they are to be successful. Thus, in a job evaluation assignment, it is not just enough to get a panel together to produce a points-factor scheme plan, analyse and evaluate benchmark jobs and devise a grade structure. The panel members must also learn how to work together in interpreting the application of a scheme in situations where roles are likely to be much more flexible than was envisaged when the original concept of points-factor job evaluation was developed.

This is an important point to bear in mind when selecting and using consultants. You do not want a firm or an individual simply to install a system in the form of a package taken from the shelf. What you really need are consultants who have the sensitivity, perception and process skills required to ensure that their system will really work within the environment and culture of a particular organisation and through the people who are involved in its operation. In other words, you want consultants who will adopt a contingency approach which ensures that their recommendations take full account of the particular circumstances of the organisation – its strategies, its product or market position and its culture.

Process consulting

Process consultants help to improve organisational effectiveness in such areas as job design (job enrichment), communications, interpersonal relationships, change management, leadership or conflict resolution. They may be involved in culture change programmes in which they initially help the organisation to redefine its values and norms concerning matters such as performance orientation, quality, customer service, innovation, flexibility, cooperative behaviour, empowerment, employee involvement or, more generally, the ways in which the organisation treats its employees.

These are the areas in which organisational development (OD) consultants used to operate. Their role could be described as making planned interventions in the processes of the organisation using behavioural science concepts, with the aim of improving organisational health and effectiveness. The term 'OD' is not used so much nowadays, perhaps because people have become somewhat cynical about the relevance or practicality of behavioural science or organisational behaviour theories. However, even if management consultants are less likely now to describe themselves as OD consultants, those who take part in the type of process consultancy projects referred to above are still likely to adopt many similar approaches.

The following are the main areas in which process consultants operate:

- *Organisation.* Overall studies may be carried out of the way in which the organisation functions and the degree to which its structure is appropriate to its mission and the competitive environment in which it operates. The process issues are likely to include how objectives and strategic plans are defined and communicated, how activities are integrated, the extent to which authority is devolved, how leadership is exercised throughout the organisation, and the overall organisation climate – the attitudes of employees to the organisation. Structural issues may include the grouping of activities, the number of layers in the organisation and the extent to which activities and decisions are centralised or decentralised.
- *Culture management/culture change.* The consultant may analyse the existing corporate culture (its norms, values and the prevailing management style), assess the degree to which the culture is appropriate, diagnose aspects of the culture which need to be changed, organise workshops and training

programmes, and help to develop management processes which will reshape or redefine values and norms and, as far as possible, provide for the behavioural modifications required for them to be acted upon.

- *Communications.* This involves conducting an audit of existing communications systems, possibly by means of an attitude survey, and advising on methods of improving communications through such means as briefing groups and the better use of the other channels of communication available such as company newsletters.
- *Total quality management (TQM).* This means gaining commitment throughout the organisation to ensure that all its activities happen the way they have been planned in order to meet the defined needs of customers and clients. The emphasis is on involving everyone in the organisation in activities which provide for continuous improvement and for achieving sustained levels of quality performance. TQM is essentially a process which makes use of a number of techniques but ultimately depends on the attitudes and behaviour of all employees. Consultants are therefore often used to help with the process aspects of the introduction of TQM as well as in helping to develop the supporting quality assurance techniques.

Training

Training services are provided by specialised training consultancies or management education establishments which deliver standard packaged courses, devise tailor-made programmes for their clients or provide guest speakers on internal training courses. All general consultancies as well as specialist HR firms and individuals are also in the business of training provision if for no other reason than that most if not all systems and process innovations have to be supported by training.

Recruitment and selection

Recruitment and selection has traditionally been one of the most thriving areas of HR consultancy. Four broad types of consultancy are provided:

- *Conventional recruitment and selection services.* These include the preparation of job and person specifications, advertising or tapping other sources, sifting applications, interviewing and testing candidates, submitting shortlists with reports on each candidate and sometimes taking part in the final selection interviews.
- *Executive search.* The consultants approach likely candidates directly but in other respects carry out broadly the same activities as conventional recruitment consultants. Executive search consultants tend to be used only for senior appointments, where there is a restricted and readily identifiable field of candidates.
- *Psychometric testing.* In addition to providing testing services, specialised consultants in this field may have developed their own tests and will also train and license clients in their use.
- *Assessment centres.* There are some consultants who specialise in the design and operation of assessment centres. They may also carry out competence analyses to produce lists of competences for use in a centre.

Many consultancies will combine more than one of these activities, some or all of which may also be provided by general firms.

Benchmarking

Benchmarking involves comparing the performance or practices of an organisation with the best practices adopted by others in the same sector or industry. This evidence is used as a basis for reviewing and, if necessary, improving what the organisation is currently doing.

Benchmarking may compare performances in such areas as productivity, service delivery, quality standards or employee turnover. It may also obtain data on the ways in which particular aspects of HR policy are applied – for example, comparing and contrasting such practices as different methods of performance appraisal, pay structures and employee benefit provisions, approaches to team pay or factory-wide incentive schemes. Consultants can help with benchmarking by making approaches to suitable organisations, analysing the results of the survey and distributing the findings to all the organisations which have participated in the programme.

3

Why and How to Use Consultants

Management consultants solve problems, produce new ideas and get things done. But a consultancy project can be expensive and time consuming, and it can fail to deliver. It is therefore essential to be quite clear in advance why you want to engage consultants and how you propose to use them. You must be reasonably certain that the benefits will justify the costs and that your resources (your own time and that of your colleagues) will be used effectively.

If consultants fail to deliver, it may be because they are not up to the job. Some consultants are better than others, some are better at doing certain things than others, and there are some charlatans and cowboys in the field – anyone can call himself or herself a consultant. It is therefore a case of *caveat emptor*. You are the buyer of consultancy services; you have to beware of the possibility that you may not get what you expect.

Professional consultants do not wilfully deceive their prospective clients, although they will naturally present themselves in the best light. Consultants may produce new CVs for each new client, which highlight appropriate experience. This is perfectly legitimate, but you should take care to establish that this experience is as appropriate as it seems. You need to find out, by asking questions and taking up references, whether the consultants are capable of delivering what is promised. And the cowboys, of course, *will* set out to deceive – they are few and far between but you still have to watch out for them.

Assignments can also fail to meet expectations because those expectations are unrealistic; the client expects too much from the consultant or the consultant fails to understand the brief. But it is again up to you to be realistic and to ensure that consultants understand what is expected of them – the 'deliverables' set out in the terms of reference.

The reasons why assignments can go wrong and what can be done if they do are explored more thoroughly in Chapter 12.

However, one of the most important factors leading to such failures, which needs to be discussed now, is a lack of understanding of why consultants should be used. If you can establish this clearly in the first place, you are much more likely to develop sensible terms of reference, form reasonable expectations of what can be achieved and select a consultant who will meet these expectations.

The main reasons for using management consultants are that:

- they provide expertise not available within the organisation;
- the provide an independent, objective and disinterested point of view;
- they have the time and resources to concentrate on the matter in hand;
- they have access to wider sources of information;
- they can act as an 'extra pair of hands'.

Each of these reasons is discussed in detail below.

Provision of expertise

An expert is someone who is practised, skilful and well informed *vis-à-vis* a particular activity or discipline (or a connected range of activities and disciplines). Consultants should bring to the assignment expertise either based directly on their own experience or related to what they have learned about best practices elsewhere. They should have a wider knowledge of the practical implications of their advice based on the experience of their previous clients or their own firm. The better consultancy firms build up a database for use by their consultants and record their accumulated expertise in practice manuals.

There are two forms of expertise: subject expertise and process expertise.

Subject expertise

As the term implies, subject expertise involves knowledge of a particular discipline or subject area. Of course, the depth and range of this expertise will vary widely from consultant to

19

consultant. A claim to expertise may be based on nothing more substantial than the fact that the consultant has read one or two seminal books or articles and packaged them as a consultancy product. There is of course nothing wrong with packaging – it is a proper marketing device and consultants are, after all, in the business of selling their services. But there has to be a legitimate product around which the packaging is wrapped and this will not be the case if the consultants have just recycled someone else's ideas. Good consultants must be articulate but bad ones can become glib as they extol the virtues of a particular panacea.

This lack of professionalism is, however, rare. Good consultants will have built up their expertise not only by following the development of new concepts but also by closely analysing their own experience and the way in which these new ideas fit or complement what they have learned and can therefore be put to good use. Expertise is also developed through research, and this is where the academics and some of the larger or more specialised consultancies benefit. It is always worthwhile asking consultants who claim to be experts to substantiate this claim, if it has not already been substantiated.

There are two kinds of subject expertise: conceptual expertise – an understanding of the nature of things in a particular discipline or field; and applied expertise – an understanding of the state of the art or best practice. The two are closely linked and both can be developed by research and analysis. Perhaps the best sort of expertise is one which has a strong conceptual base upon which an understanding of best practice is based. However, it should be remembered that best practice must be carefully defined. It is what is likely to be the best practice in *particular* circumstances, based on the practices that have worked well in *similar* circumstances.

Process expertise

Process expertise is concerned with the approaches and techniques used by consultants in planning and conducting assignments. Process expertise will cover such areas as:

- the ability to discern the real issues presented by a prospective

20

client and to turn this understanding into a convincing proposal which defines realistic expectations about deliverables;
- project management – the ability to plan and control an assignment so that expectations are fulfilled within a predetermined time scale and cost budget;
- process counselling – the ability to understand the processes at work in the client's organisation and apply this understanding to the production of worthwhile and acceptable recommendations;
- the ability to present proposals and recommendations convincingly not only to you as the sponsor but also to anyone else in the organisation who is concerned with the outcome of the assignment.

Use of expertise

Subject expertise is no use without process expertise, and vice versa. When selecting consultants you should be certain that the firm or individual can supply both. In large assignments a firm may deliberately select a balanced team of consultants with a mix of both types. Team leaders (managing consultants) are often selected because of their strengths in the process area and their ability to deploy the subject expertise of their team and their firm effectively.

Obviously, the decision to use consultants as experts is based on the assumption that the expertise required is not available within the organisation. However, as we shall see in Chapter 4, this assumption needs to be challenged.

Independence and objectivity

Consultants can be engaged simply because there is a need for a problem to be addressed by someone who will not be bound, influenced or prejudiced by organisational norms and traditions, politics or any other internal factors which may hinder a solution – someone who can see the wood for the trees.

Consultants are (or should be) objective in that they base their conclusions and recommendations on a rigorous process of analysis and diagnosis. They should not be diverted by half-baked assumptions and they ought to be able to withstand the pressure of special interest groups and people with axes to grind. They should also be disinterested. Effective consultants do not allow personal considerations to affect the advice they give. They may be aware of the fact that their recommendations can lead to further implementation or follow-up work, but if they are professional in their approach, this consideration should not be allowed to influence recommendations.

One example of the use of consultants to provide independent advice has resulted from the Cadbury report on company boards. The report recommended that board remuneration committees should base their deliberations on hard data about levels of rewards and benefits for company directors. This information is increasingly being provided by consultants who specialise in carrying out studies of directors' pay. Chief executives have also been known to enlist the help of management consultants to support their own claims for higher pay by producing evidence of what the 'going rate' is for similar jobs.

They can also often be called in by chief executives to consider the views of different factions on how to deal with a problem or the best way forward. The hope is that the consultants will provide dispassionate advice which will avoid compromise and lead to a properly integrated solution.

Another situation in which the detachment and objectivity of management consultants is often used is the review of organisational structures. This is an area where some people will be fighting to maintain the status quo, while others will be advocating changes which could well be as beneficial to them as to the organisation. There is never one right solution to such studies and it often needs an outsider to cut through the web of competing ideas and come up with practical and acceptable solutions.

HR directors may want the disinterested support of consultants to develop and implement such systems or processes as a new pay structure, performance management or a performance-related pay scheme. There may be a number of different views within the organisation on what should be done and how, and it is often thought that the weight of authority provided by an independent consultant may carry the day if there are differences of opinion. It can, however, appear to be a sign of weakness if you have to seek expensive outside help simply to back up your own ideas.

The problem is that many clients have a natural tendency to believe that whoever pays the piper calls the tune. Good consultants will be prepared to resist this pressure whenever it is against the longer-term interests of their client.

Concentration

External consultants are often used because they can concentrate on the matter in hand. They should be working to firm terms of reference with defined deliverables and deadlines, and are not distracted by the day-to-day pressures of decision making and routine administration.

This advantage can be invalidated, however, if, in the interests of economy, they are put under too much pressure to cut short the time they spend on the assignment. Both clients and consultants can be at fault in this respect. Clients cannot expect consultants to operate effectively within time constraints that are too tight. Consultants can of course resist such pressures but it can sometimes be difficult for them to argue the case for more time; estimating the time required for an assignment is an art rather than a science.

Some consultants may also be tempted to cut corners to get an assignment or to keep one going. This is clearly an undesirable practice, and the client and consultant should agree realistic time and cost parameters from the outset. Consultants should be able to define what you will get for your money. If you want more you will have to pay for it. Once this budget has been fixed it should only be altered by mutual agreement if there has been a change in circumstances. If, for example, cash-flow problems mean that you do not have the money to pay for the full programme of work you should agree a change in the terms of reference which still allows the consultant a reasonable amount of time to do a good job.

Before engaging consultants, it is also worth checking that they are not going to be too distracted by competing demands on their time. It is a temptation for independent consultants to take on extra clients whenever they are offered the opportunity because they may not be sure when the next assignment will come. As a client, it is wise to establish in advance that the consultant will be able to devote the time and energy required.

This problem can also arise in larger firms where operating consultants may be assigned to more than one client if they cannot be allocated full time, and managing consultants may be controlling a number of different assignments. In such cases the consultants may be faced with conflicting priorities. Again, good consultants will be capable of doing this, but it is necessary for clients to be aware of the fact that sorting out priorities can sometimes be a problem.

One of the qualities of effective consultants is that they are able to focus on the real issues and allocate their time accordingly. As a client, you must give them sufficient scope to do this. You should not spend your time breathing down their neck, insisting that they work in accordance with your perceptions of the priorities. Consultants are paid to get this right. If you do have real doubts, bring your reservations out into the open in good time. Assignments can all too easily go off the rails if remedial action is not taken promptly.

Access to information

Experienced consultants should have access to a wide range of information in their discipline, based on their own experience, the experience of their firm and, it is to be hoped, the application of a programme of continuous development.

They will have access to unpublished information and as independent organisations they may be better placed to conduct benchmarking surveys.

An 'extra pair of hands'

You may feel that you have the expertise, the objectivity and the ability to concentrate to get the job done, but you may simply not have the time or resources required. HR professionals have priority problems like everyone else – indeed more than most people if they are at the beck and call of all their internal clients. They sometimes have to place a desirable innovation on the 'back burner' because there are too many issues to which they have to give their immediate attention. In these circumstances it is tempting to bring in consultants simply to get the job done more quickly. It is, however, a costly temptation and one that you may well have to resist. The calculation is based on relative cost-effectiveness. For example, would it be more effective for you to spend your time on a long-range career planning or management development programme, or should you devote your energies to administer all the stages of a recruitment exercise to fill an immediate vacancy? Recruitment and selection is, in fact, an area in which it is relatively easy to justify the engagement of consultants. You are no doubt perfectly capable of doing it yourself, but it is very time-consuming going through all the stages, and it can be tedious . Recruitment consultants will not necessarily do it better than you, but they will at least free you for more productive activities.

Similar considerations may arise in a number of other areas of HR management. You may, for example, want help with the job analysis part of a job evaluation assignment, or with the considerable work involved in developing competency definitions, or with planning and contributing to an internal management training course. Whether or not you will engage the 'extra pair of hands' will depend on the extent to which you can justify the additional costs involved.

As I said in the Introduction, one factor encouraging this use of consultants is the slimming down of many personnel departments, which means that they have to rely more on outside help to get their projects completed.

Conclusions

Any one of the above reasons may be sufficient to justify the use of management consultants; in most cases more than one or even all of them may be valid. But it is necessary to be quite clear in your mind about which of them applies in your case before beginning the process of identifying the need as discussed in the next chapter.

It is also necessary, however, to consider very carefully whether you can do the job yourself, by setting up an internal project team or using internal consultants. If you do it yourself, you will at least know from personal experience what people inside the organisation are capable of doing, whereas unless you have used an external consultant before, anyone you engage will always be something of an unknown quantity, however carefully you select them. It is often not so much a matter of expertise as the extent to which the outsider will fit the organisation, something you may only find out when you use them. Further consideration is given to the use of internal consultants in Chapter 12.

If, after considering the alternatives, you still believe that external consultants will provide added value you should consider the different ways of using them. At one extreme, a full-blown consultancy assignment may involve a team of consultants under a team leader carrying out the whole process of analysis, diagnosis, formulation of proposals and implementation. Or they may only be involved up to the implementation stage, leaving you to put their recommendations into effect.

At the other extreme, you may simply invite consultants to provide an input into your thinking – either at the beginning of a project to provide you with ideas to develop, or in its concluding stages, when you can test your conclusions against their knowledge and experience. Such inputs can take the form of seminars or workshops for a project team, providing its members with additional stimulus.

Between these extremes you can reduce the involvement of consultants if your own staff or members of a project team carry out some of the work which a consultant might do. For example, the most time-consuming element of a job evaluation assignment is job analysis. To analyse one job and produce an agreed job or role description may take several hours. It may be possible for your staff to carry out these analyses once they have been trained by a consultant, who could also monitor progress and exercise quality control. Another approach would be to appoint a consultant as an advisor to a project team or a group of internal consultants. The external consultant would give the team the benefit of his or her ideas and provide periodic guidance during the project. The team might ask the consultant to become involved in some aspects of the project, but the team itself would do most of the work.

----------4----------

Establishing What You Need

The first step you need to take in using consultants effectively is clearly to establish the need. The points to be considered are:

- how the need for a consultancy project may arise;
- how to identify the need;
- whether or not this is a consultancy project;
- whether to use external or internal consultants;
- how to define the objectives and the programme of work for an assignment;
- what the costs are likely to be;
- how to persuade higher authority that the need exists;
- how to assess the likely reactions of managers, employees and trade unions (if any).

How the need may arise

The following are some examples of the types of consultancy projects that I have initiated or been associated with during my career in personnel management:

- a review of the reasons for the heavy losses of newly recruited graduates in their first two years and ways of reducing them;
- the engagement of executive search consultants on a number of occasions;
- the implementation of a craft apprentice selection scheme using a battery of psychometric and attainment tests;
- the introduction of team briefing and quality circles;
- the development of a group incentive scheme for warehouse staff;
- the development of a new pay structure for managers in a publishing company;
- the development of a maturity curve pay system for research and development engineers;

- a review of the reasons for wage drift in a factory incentive scheme and ways of improving the scheme itself and the working arrangements;
- the introduction of the Hay system of job evaluation;
- the development of a new system of performance management;
- an assessment of the potential benefits of the Government's profit-related pay scheme;
- the construction of an entirely new pensions scheme following a takeover.

The need for consultancy may therefore arise for a variety of reasons, including: a significant change in the circumstances or technology of the organisation, a major problem in the employment or development of people or in employee relations, or the perceived requirement for a new approach or innovation in some aspect of HRM.

The impact of change

A takeover or merger may mean that important changes have to be made to the structure of the organisation or to the terms and conditions of employment it offers its staff, or both. There may be a need for down-sizing or recruitment, either to replace key individuals who have left as a result of the takeover or to fill newly created positions.

Alternatively, technological change such as the introduction of computerised integrated manufacturing systems or new information technology networks may require the development of new skills or the acquisition of people who have the necessary skills.

A major general consultancy exercise such as the newly fashionable business process re-engineering studies may also lead to massive organisational changes. Such exercises start from scratch, examining and challenging everything that is currently done and replacing or removing superfluous or unprofitable activities, changing structures and roles and down-sizing as necessary. Such drastic changes may create a need for new employment and reward procedures and systems.

The need for innovation or changes in HR policies and practices may also be initiated by a significant change in the role of the organisation. This may take place when a Government department becomes an agency or a nationalised industry is privatised. Typically, these lead at least to new reward structures, often incorporating performance-related pay if this did not already exist. New performance management systems are also frequently introduced in these circumstances.

Another reason for changes in personnel systems or procedures may be a strategic review which initiates new product or market developments. Relocations and start-ups may require a completely new approach to the provision of personnel services or to employee relations policies.

Problems

The problems which might create a need for a consultancy project include poor levels of performance or productivity, operational inflexibility, poor morale, lack of commitment, high employee turnover, difficulties in attracting and retaining high-quality people, an inadequate or diminishing skills base, an inequitable pay structure, a crumbling job evaluation scheme, an expensive and over-complex employee benefit structure, poor leadership, inadequate teamwork or a poor climate of employee relations.

A different sort of problem arises when you know perfectly well what needs to be done, as with a recruitment or training programme, but lack the time or resources to do it.

The need for innovation

HRM should be a proactive as well as a reactive process. Most of the negative feelings about the concept of HRM expressed by those reared in the old traditions of personnel management is caused by the fact that HRM is usually defined as being owned and driven by line management. Where, say some personnel professionals, does this leave us? Are we simply here to administer recruitment, pay, training, personnel records and the canteen, provide advice on employment law and police the implementation of personnel policies? Or do we still have a wider role? The answer, of course, is that they do. Their role is to be alert to the

29

ever-changing and developing needs of the organisation and to provide whatever guidance is required to ensure that it makes the best use of its human resources. They may sometimes have to exercise pressure, intervening as necessary to suggest new approaches and to take part in their development and implementation. HR professionals have an important innovatory role as well as being service providers. And the innovations should be aimed at improving the organisation's effectiveness through its people.

Identifying the need

There will be many occasions when the need for a consultancy project is obvious following a major change or crisis. On other occasions symptoms of a problem may be apparent, such as high employee turnover or low productivity, but the cause would have to be investigated before a possible need for a consultancy project could be identified.

As mentioned earlier, one of the key roles of HR specialists is to intervene when they believe that something is going wrong or when they feel that there is scope for innovation or improvement. The search for areas where innovation is likely to have beneficial results can never be relaxed. It may be carried out passively by simply keeping one's eyes open and one's ears close to the ground. More positively, it can be conducted by going around and talking and listening to people at all levels in the organisation.

It is necessary to know what the organisation's success criteria are and to study the performance indicators which will reveal the extent to which they are being met. You should look behind the figures (the symptoms) to get at the causes and the potential need for action. Attitude surveys can be used periodically to identify problem areas. An audit approach can also be used to evaluate each aspect of HRM practice.

It is important at this stage to sound out the reactions of those who might be affected by the project. These will include your boss, your colleagues, members of your department and other employees and their representatives. If you have used an attitude survey you will have obtained some idea of the areas in which their reaction is likely to be favourable. But if you have trade unions it is particularly important to obtain some reaction from them in advance, preferably on an informal basis. Trade unions can be understandably hostile to any proposal for consultancy which they think may affect the interests of their members or may prejudice their position. They can, for example, be suspicious of innovations which may seem innocuous to the employer, such as job evaluation, performance appraisal, performance-rated pay and quality circles.

Is this a consultancy project?

Once you have established a need to do something, you must decide whether it is a consultancy project. Could it not be accomplished as part of the normal processes of management rather than being set up as a separate entity? Or could it be handled as an internal consultancy project? The distinction is not always clear and there is often an element of choice.

There are clearly advantages and disadvantages in all three approaches. Doing it yourself may be the easiest option: there are no additional costs and you will be in complete control. On the other hand there may be opportunity costs in using outsiders: you could spend your time more profitably doing other things. Moreover, your ideas may be more acceptable if they are backed up by the opinions of other people. You may also have to be prepared to admit, at least to yourself, that you lack the necessary experience and expertise to carry the project through. And you may not have access to the wide range of information on good practice which consultants should possess.

A project team approach has the advantage of spreading the load and bringing in a wider range of contributions from individuals, all with a knowledge of the organisation and its problems. The support of someone acting in an internal consultancy capacity would considerably strengthen the team. But project teams can be inbred and unadventurous, and it may not be possible for their members to give the project the attention it deserves. There is also no guarantee that even the collective experience of an internal project team would be sufficient to tackle a demanding project requiring a considerable amount of innovative thinking. The advantages of using external consultants were set out in Chapter 3. They can work well with members of the organisation, thus combining the advantages of the collective effort of a project team with those of external expertise and independence. But they can be expensive and there is always the risk that, however analytical and objective they may be, they will not get to grips with the particular problems and culture of your organisation. It should be remembered that the degree to which consultants can be involved can vary considerably – from taking full responsibility for all aspects of the project at one extreme to simply providing a valuable input to the thinking of the team at appropriate stages in the assignment at the other.

Internal or external consultants?

The choice may be between an internal or external consultancy approach. If you take on the project yourself, whether you are acting on your own or with a project team, you will in effect be an internal consultant. If your organisation is facing the continuous need to innovate in particular areas of HRM, such as HR development, you may consider appointing one or more people as internal consultants or identifying individuals in other departments who can carry out this role. The use of internal consultants is discussed in detail in Chapter 12.

Defining objectives

When you have decided that a consultancy project is required and established the extent to which you want to use external consultants, you should set down what you want the assignment to achieve and the benefits that should accrue to the organisation. These could be expressed as improved performance, productivity and profitability – the three Ps – and no consultancy assignment should be undertaken unless you are convinced that it will add value in any or all of these areas.

A definition of the objectives and benefits of a performance management assignment, for example, might read:

> To introduce a process of performance management covering all employees which will be based on the agreement of objectives and required competence levels leading to an assessment of contribution and competence against the agreed objectives and competences.
>
> The introduction of performance management is intended to improve individual and team and therefore organisational performance by:
>
> - clarifying roles, objectives and competence requirements;
> - focusing attention on key performance issues;
> - identifying areas of poor performance or lack of competence and correcting them;
> - building a sound foundation for the development and improvement of performance and competence.

This definition provides a basis for considering what work will be required, how much it might cost and how the project will be presented to higher authority and discussed with employees and trade unions.

The most difficult part of any consultancy project is thinking it through sufficiently at the outset to be able to define it clearly, so that it gains the approval of management, helps in discussions with employees and provides a good basis for preparing a brief for consultants.

The process of defining objectives can be facilitated by drafting a one-sentence decision statement in the form of 'We want to decide X.' For example, if your pay structure is inequitable, uncompetitive and based on inadequate processes of job evaluation, you might produce a decision statement along the lines of:

> We want to decide: first, how to introduce an analytical process of job evaluation which will enable us to manage relativities more fairly and consistently; secondly, how to analyse market rates; and thirdly, how to design a more competitive pay structure.

You would also need to consider the potential benefits of doing this in such terms as reducing staff dissatisfaction and turnover, preventing grade drift (unjustified upgradings), easing the problems of administering the system, providing equal pay for work of equal value and producing a logical pay structure within which appropriate internal and external relativities can be maintained and which establishes a good basis for introducing performance-related pay.

You should, however, go further and try to assess the overall benefits to the organisation in such terms as increasing productivity and profitability, improving performance, reducing costs, adding value, achieving sustainable competitive advantage and generally adding to the bottom line.

Ideally you should place yourself in a position where you do a cost/benefit analysis as a basis for justifying the assignment. However, while you may be able to quantify costs reasonably well (both of the consultants' fees and of implementing their recommendations), it may be much more difficult to quantify benefits. For example, it may be assumed that a performance-related pay system will improve performance but experience has shown that it is difficult to calculate with any precision what its impact will be. However, the attempt should be made. You are likely, in practice, to be in a better position to estimate total costs and benefits when you have received and discussed proposals from consultants.

Work required

You need at this stage to prepare some preliminary ideas about the work required. This will provide the basis for a rough estimate of costs, for your submission to higher authority and for your assessment of the consultant's proposals.

You could form a view about work requirements from your previous experience, by reading the relevant literature, by talking to other HR people who have conducted a similar project and possibly by sounding out consultants you know without committing yourself to engaging them.

The stages in a programme of work for a job evaluation assignment might be as follows, assuming that you decide on a tailor-made scheme rather than a consultancy firm's 'proprietary brand', and also that you decide to extend the objectives to include a market rate survey.

1. Do preliminary work – data collection and detailed programming.
2. Set up and brief project team.
3. Develop factor plan for points-factor job evaluation scheme.
4. Select, analyse and evaluate benchmark jobs.
5. Develop grade structure.
6. Evaluate and grade remaining jobs.
7. Conduct market rate survey.
8. Define pay ranges.
9. Determine methods of pay progression within ranges.
10. Communicate results to staff.

Estimating costs

If you need to seek approval for a consultancy assignment it is advisable to have some idea of the likely costs. These will depend on four factors.

- the extent to which you intend to use consultants;
- the amount of work to be done;
- the consultant's fee rates and the expenses they will incur;
- the cost of implementing the consultant's recommendations.

The extent to which external consultants are to be used

This may be a matter of choice. Consultants' costs can be reduced considerably if you, your staff or members of a project team carry out some of the data collection and analytical work and if you do not seek any help with implementation.

The volume of work

It may be easy in a straightforward assignment such as training provision to estimate how much time a consultant will need to prepare and deliver a session on a course or to run a workshop. And in some situations you may decide in advance precisely how much time you want a consultant to spend in providing advice or conducting analytical work.

35

In the case of more complex projects it may be more difficult. If you have already lined up a consultant you will be able to obtain an estimate of the time and costs involved. But you may not have selected a consultant or even wish to approach one until you have obtained internal clearance for the project, and in this case you have to attempt to make a rough estimate yourself. You could do this by referring to the programme of work you have drawn up and assessing how much time a consultant might have to spend at each stage, allowing for some internal contribution. For example, the estimate for the job evaluation project described earlier could be built up as follows:

Stage	Consultant days
1. Preliminary discussions data collection and detailed programming	2
2. Setting up and briefing project team	1
3. Developing factor plan	2
4. Selecting, analysing and evaluating benchmark jobs (assuming that much of this work will be done by the project team)	8
5. Developing grade structure	2
6. Evaluating and grading remaining jobs jobs (most of this to be done by the project team)	5
7. Conducting market rate survey (analysing published data only)	3
8. Defining pay ranges	2

9. Determining methods for pay progression   4
   and the administration of the system

10. Preparing communication to staff   1
                                                  ___
                                                  30
                                                  ___

In addition, if you are contemplating the use of a large firm you may have to allow for three to five days' supervisory time.

If you have to produce the time estimates yourself, without the advice of an experienced consultant, you should remember that they are likely to be based mainly on guesswork. If they must be revealed to other people within the organisation, therefore, you should emphasise that they are highly tentative and cannot be confirmed until the project has been discussed with consultants.

Fees and expenses

Fees vary considerably. Some consultants may charge as little as £100–200 a day, but they are often inexperienced, or are redundant executives filling in time and earning a little extra cash.

Independent consultants may charge anything from £250 to £1,000 a day, or more if they are very prestigious or are advising on major strategic issues. A rate of £500–750 a day is fairly typical for a well-established independent consultant. Academics tend to charge similar fees to independent consultants, although they are sometimes lower.

The rates charged by the larger consultancies are generally higher. An experienced consultant is likely to be charged out at between £750 and £1,000 a day, and the fees of senior or managing consultants can be as high as £1,250–1,500 a day, or even more in the case of partners or directors.

On this basis, you might assume for estimating purposes that if you use independent consultants or academics you would incur fees of £500 or so a day, plus expenses and, of course, VAT at the normal rate if they are VAT registered. If you are considering a larger firm, you might assume a rate of £750 for a 'resident' consultant and, if it is a large assignment, extra costs for supervision at, say, £1,000 a day. Thus the costs of the job evaluation

37

assignment referred to above could be estimated at £15,000 if an independent consultant were used and £25,000 if a large firm were engaged (although the rates of a large firm could be considerably higher, depending on the nature of the work and the level of consultant employed). You might be able to negotiate a reduction in the larger firms' fees, but the difference in rates given above is fairly typical. Of course, what you are paying for in the larger firm is reputation and back-up – it will have research services, quality assurance procedures, consultancy support staff and additional consulting resources that are out of the reach of the typical independent consultant. The factors to be taken into account in making this choice are explored in the next chapter.

In this example, therefore, you could produce an estimate of up to £25,000, plus expenses. But it must be re-emphasised that these calculations will always be highly tentative at this stage and the example is based on assumptions about fee rates which may vary considerably. You should be very cautious about quoting such estimates to any colleagues.

The cost of implementation

The costs of implementing the recommendations arising from a consultancy project would cover such items as training, additional staff, new equipment or software. It may be extremely difficult to estimate these at this stage unless you are absolutely clear what the outcome of the project will be – which is unlikely in most cases. You will be in a better position to do this when you have studied and discussed the consultant's proposals. Meanwhile, you may have to be content with making a mental note that these costs may arise and should be taken into account in calculating the overall costs and benefits of the assignment.

Gaining agreement to a project

You may possibly have a budget for consultancy, especially for training and recruitment, and by exercising considerable powers of persuasion at budgeting time, HR directors have been known to acquire a consultancy contingency fund which they can use more or less at their discretion (although it is always advisable to clear a consultancy project in advance with those likely to be affected by it).

HR directors and their staff may also be involved in aspects of a general consultancy project which has been set up by the chief executive or the board. In these circumstances, it is to be hoped that the HR director will have taken part in defining the terms of reference for any project with HR implications and will both be involved in selecting the consultants and act as a member of a steering group or project team.

If this is your project, however, and you have no budget to cover it, you will have to get approval from your boss or the board. Your proposal should explain why you think the project is necessary, its objectives, the terms of reference you have in mind and the benefits you believe it will produce. If appropriate, you should refer to the likely reactions of employees and trade unions, which you should try to assess in advance. This aspect is discussed in more detail at the end of the chapter. It goes without saying that it is sometimes best to use a 'softening-up' approach, gradually unfolding the problem or need over a series of discussions or meetings and building up the case for solving it by using consultants. In my experience, springing a major project on someone out of the blue, whether that someone is a chief executive, an HR director or a union representative, can sometimes produce an instinctive negative reaction.

In formulating your proposal you will need to anticipate objections, the most likely of which will be: 'Why don't you do this yourself – that is what you're paid for after all.' It may not be expressed as crudely as that but it is a fairly common reaction. Other negative reactions which you may have to anticipate include:

- 'I agree it is important to do something, but this is not the right time to do it.'
- 'Surely there is a simple solution to this problem – why bother with a consultant?'
- 'We'll never get the staff/the trade unions to accept this idea.'
- 'I don't believe in using consultants; once you get them in you can't get rid of them.'
- 'I know all about using consultants – they come up with slick solutions and then leave you to sort out the mess.'

- 'It will take up too much of my/your/our time.'
- 'Are you sure we will get value for money?'
- 'It will cost too much.'

The last two objections may be the most difficult to deal with. This is because, as I said earlier, except in the most basic or straightforward assignments, it is very difficult to anticipate at this stage just how much a consultancy project will cost.

You can avoid this problem by obtaining one or more firm estimates from consultants before putting your proposition to your boss or the board, but this could waste time and there may be negative reactions from above if you are perceived to have gone too far without authority.

In my experience, when you are unsure of the exact costs the best approach is to ask for agreement in principle, subject to approval of its likely cost after you have made further enquiries. You should have in mind some idea of the possible costs but you should try to avoid committing yourself to this estimate. You might be told that you can go ahead as long as you do not exceed a certain figure, and this would provide a perfectly reasonable base for proceeding. If after obtaining estimates it is quite clear that the job cannot be done satisfactorily within the budget you can always put forward a case for the budget to be increased. Try to avoid being placed in a position of working within a tight budget when you believe that the project cannot be completed satisfactorily for that amount.

Assessing likely reactions

As I have said, the importance of assessing likely reactions to any project which may affect managers and the terms and conditions of employees cannot be overemphasised. This can be done fairly informally, although in some circumstances it might be advisable to raise the matter formally with trade unions. You will need to anticipate their reactions when setting up, conducting and implementing the project and it will be necessary at this stage to consider the extent to which you want to involve them as members of a project team or whether you will have to bow to their insistence on being involved.

If trade union representatives are involved, they may reserve the right to take part in discussions but not to agree to any conclusions the consultant or the project team has reached without seeking the views of their members.

5

Sourcing Consultants

There are five main types of consultancies or consultants:

- The large multi-discipline consultancy firms, which include general consultancies like PE and PA and the accountancy firms such as Coopers & Lybrand, KPMG Peat Marwick, Price Waterhouse and Ernst Young who have long-established consultancy divisions.
- The specialist firms in HR as a whole or in some area of HR such as pay, recruitment, testing, training or what may broadly be called organisational development. The smaller, highly specialised firms are sometimes known as 'boutiques'. Some firms specialise in a sector – niche consulting. For example, Compass and CR Consultants operate in the voluntary sector.
- The small firms or independent consultants (sole practitioners), who may provide a range of services or may specialise in one area such as recruitment or training. Independent consultants may be part of a network, which may be very informal or fairly structured with a central office to provide support activities and direct work to, subscribers. This category includes individuals, often redundant or retired executives, who will act as consultants to fill in time before they find a job or to keep themselves occupied.
- Academics who carry out occasional consulting work in addition to their research and teaching activities. These are often based in business schools or management training institutions such as Ashridge College and Henley Management College.
- Organisations which provide HR consultancy services as part of their other activities, such as ACAS and the Industrial Society.

Advantages and disadvantages of different types of consultant

Large general firms

From the point of view of sourcing potential HR consultants the distinction between large general companies and large accountancy-based firms is not significant. They will both have divisions or sub-divisions concentrating on various aspects of management such as finance, IT, strategic studies, marketing, production and HR, and these divisions will be staffed by professionals in the various disciplines.

A large firm will have an established reputation and a lot of experience in the field. It will be able to attract high-quality graduates and professional staff and will aim mainly to recruit people who have had some years' practical experience, generally in a sophisticated environment. They may also recruit graduates straight from universities or business schools as assistant or trainee consultants, on the grounds that what they may lack in practical experience will be more than compensated for by their quality and their level of education. In recent years there has been a tendency for some of the best graduates to go into consultancy rather than to pursue an academic career.

The large firms will take great care over the selection of consultants, often using assessment centres. They will take even greater care over the training of new staff in consultancy techniques, both in formal courses and by close supervision from more senior consultants. They will have practice manuals which encapsulate the knowledge they have gained over the years.

Until they have proved themselves, inexperienced consultants will be closely supervised. They may be employed mainly in analytical or back-up research as junior members of a team. Even highly experienced consultants will be subject to quite close quality control from more senior members of the firm. In large assignments there may be a hierarchy of control downwards from a partner or director through managing or senior consultants to the operating or resident consultants. This control will be concerned with quality assurance and project management to ensure the success of an assignment both from the client's point of view (achieving its terms of reference within budget and attaining project objectives) and from the point of view of the consultancy firm (adding to its range of experience and reputation, building good client relations in the expectation of further work and, of course, making a profit).

Large firms will have a data bank of experience to which consultants can refer, together with internal support services for the production of graphics and slides. Some firms spend considerable sums on research and product development. They will pride themselves, usually with justification, on the analytical and diagnostic ability of their consultants and you can normally expect highly professional, well written, closely argued and clearly presented proposals and reports from them. Their consultants will have been specially trained in presentational skills and often in the art of running workshops and process consultancy.

A criticism that used to be levelled at the large consultancy firms was that a high-powered consultant would be involved in selling the services of the firm to the client and would then disappear to sell elsewhere, leaving an unknown and somewhat less high-powered consultant in the field. This no longer happens, if it ever did. If a senior consultant is involved in preparing the initial proposal he or she will run the project and the client will be asked to agree in advance the amount of supervisory time that should be included in the fee. Managing or senior consultants are likely, of course, to be involved in much more than simply supervising the field consultant. They may be responsible for the more strategic aspects of the assignment as well as taking part in key initial and 'milestone' meetings to discuss approaches and findings. They may become even more involved in the concluding stages of the assignment to add value to the final conclusions and recommendations. It is worth noting that, although many of the large consultancies attach ranks to their consultants (and some are quite hierarchical), the roles of people at different levels can change quite significantly, depending on the nature of the assignment. Thus a partner or director may play a major role as a consultant in a top-level or stategic assignment, and more junior consultants might simply provide support to that partner rather than operating independently.

The advantages of large firms can be summed up as being the breadth and depth of their experience, the quality of their consultants as a result of careful selection and systematic training, their quality assurance and project management processes and expertise, and the back-up they give their consultants in the field.

Large consultancies are sometimes accused of being impersonal, not looking after the interests of smaller clients. Neither of these accusations is true. There is no essential difference between the role of an operating or resident consultant from a big firm and that of an independent consultant or a member of a smaller firm. In each case the main and most immediate relationship is between the client and the consultant, not the client and the firm. Indeed, with a larger firm, contacts may be made with more senior consultants but these are still personal and related directly to the project. And the larger firms are as interested in getting business as anyone and are not going to reject the opportunity of an assignment with a small organisation, although they are naturally looking mainly for big assignments and repeat business from their key clients.

It is true, however, that large firms may have had less experience in dealing with small clients, and there is sometimes a tendency for them to assign their less experienced consultants to such engagements, although they will still be supervised carefully – it is not in their interests to provide poor service to any clients, whatever their size. Ultimately it is up to you to ensure that you are satisfied with the quality of the consultant who is being assigned to your project. If inexperienced consultants are put forward you can challenge their ability to do the job and insist that, while they may provide support in the fact-finding and analytical aspects of the assignment, you expect a more experienced consultant be responsible for the project.

Larger consultancies can also be expensive. Their rates may be 50 per cent or more higher than those charged by most independent consultants. But there will always be exceptions – some independent consultants charge more, some large firms charge less, while some firms have differential fee scales, depending on the level of work they are doing.

The reasons for these high fees are fairly obvious. They have to pay their consultants well because of the level of ability and expertise they need to attract and retain, and because consultants expect a good reward for the considerable demands made on them. They generally have high overheads, including the cost of training, research and maintaining their database.

Specialist firms

The main advantage of specialist firms is that their expertise and competences will be focused on HR – or on an area of HR – rather than being dispersed over a number of disciplines. They can use their experience to develop their particular techniques and build up a data bank of information on best practice.

The HR departments in the larger general firms will argue that they do exactly the same because they exist as separate entities in the firm, a point which is hard to deny. However, specialist firms would maintain that by concentrating on a particular field over a number of years and by attracting the best specialists in that field, they have created a level of expertise and an understanding of the state of the art that generalists are unable to match. This is a judgement which can only be put to the test by asking both types of firm to tender for an assignment and by comparing their respective philosophies and approaches and the quality of staff they will be able to assign to the project.

Small firms and independent consultants

Small firms and independent consultants can provide specific expertise, often at significantly lower rates than the larger general or specialised consultants. But it should always be remembered that it is the total cost that counts, not the rate at which they charge, and a larger firm may be able to deliver the results required at a lower cost, even if its fees are higher.

Smaller firms often claim that 'small is beautiful' and that they will be able to provide a much more personal and attentive service than a large consultancy. However, there is no reason why a larger firm should not be just as attentive and focused on the needs of a client as a small firm or a sole practitioner.

It is quite possible, however, that a member of a small firm or a sole practitioner will have the particular sort of expertise, understanding and experience you are looking for. If you approach a larger firm, *they* will choose the consultant they intend to assign to the project, unless you make a particular request for someone you know. With a small firm or an independent consultant you know who you are going to get from the start. If you understand what you are looking for you will be in a better position to achieve a good fit – matching the consultant to the project and to your organisation – and that is a vital ingredient for the success of any assignment.

On the other hand small firms and independent consultants will not have the back-up resources and extensive data banks possessed by the larger general or specialist firms, although they can make up for this by providing concentrated experience and expertise.

There is a tendency for larger organisations to engage larger consultancy firms, either because of the scale of the project, or on the basis of their track record, reputation and resources. They may also be activated by the belief that it takes a large organisation to understand a larger organisation, although there is no foundation for this belief. The result is that members of a small firm or an independent consultant may lack large-organisation consultancy experience, unless they have previously worked in a big firm. However, there are many examples of highly effective and experienced independent consultants being used successfully by large firms where their particular expertise fits the need.

Academics

Academics, either working independently or as members of a team from their institution, are being used increasingly as consultants. Individual academics are sought because of the reputation they have built up through their research, publications and platform appearances. They can bring their knowledge of their subject and their well-honed analytical and diagnostic skills to the job. Moreover if they have been involved in research they may have developed a deeper understanding of the real issues of HR management than a management consultant who has to concentrate on the matter in hand and might not be able to pay as much attention to these wider concerns (although good consultants *will* do this, which is one reason why they are good consultants).

Academics will have observed by research what does and does not work, and one of the benefits they can bring to an organisation is a healthy agnostic view about the prescriptions for organisational effectiveness offered by some popular writers on the subject and by some consultants.

47

Many academics like to carry out consultancy projects because it puts them more closely in touch with real management problems, and provides useful case-study material and additional research data. All this can benefit their clients as well as themselves.

The risk you may run in engaging some (but by no means all) academics is that their role is to teach and to carry out research. Their primary purpose is not to provide a consultancy service and they may not have the skills which a professional consultant will have developed to help their clients turn concepts and the results of analytical studies and diagnoses into practical courses of action. 'Prescriptive' is a dirty word for many academics, but consultants are inevitably placed in positions where they are expected to prescribe for their clients. They will take care to ensure that the prescription is developed jointly by the client and themselves and is not delivered by them on tablets of stone as the only answer. But it remains a prescription not just a description based on analysis, which is what some academic research amounts to. And however interesting this may be, it will not necessarily solve a management problem.

Other organisations providing consultancy services

Organisations such as the Industrial Society and ACAS provide HR consultancy or advisory services on the same basis as the specialised consultancy firms but often at a lower cost (in the case of ACAS, sometimes at no cost at all).

Training organisations

The Training and Enterprise Councils (TECs) and other industrial or commercial training organisations will provide specialised training services, which include the analysis of training needs and the development and delivery of training programmes.

Finding consultants

If you have already used a firm or an individual consultant successfully, you may decide to use them again, as long as their experience is relevant to the new project. You know them and they know you, and this is a very satisfactory basis for a continuing relationship. You should, however, be aware of one potential danger: the relationship can become too close, and if this happens the consultant will no longer be completely disinterested – some of his or her objectivity will have been sacrificed. You should also be aware of the danger of becoming too dependent on consultants, although a good consultant will take pains to avoid this situation.

If you have no direct knowledge of a consultant you will have to rely on recommendations, registers such as the ones operated by the Institute of Personnel Management (IPM) and the Management Consultancy Information Service (MCIS) or the directories of consultants whose addresses are given in the Appendix. You can also study advertisements in the personnel journals. The problem of course is that while you may know something about the major general or specialist firms, there are thousands of small firms and independent consultants about which you will know nothing. No one knows exactly how many HR consultants there are practising. The *APS Personnel Manager's Year Book* lists some 700 HR consultancies and 1,400 training organisations, and the *Directory of Management Consultants in the UK* has over 5,000 entries under the general heading of HR consultant. But there are many more consultants who are not in any register or directory.

The main sources of information are given below.

Personal recommendation

In theory this is the best way to find out about consultants, and if you have no one particular in mind it is certainly well worth your while asking around. But you need to be careful. A consultant may be recommended who has done a very good job for someone else but may not fit your circumstances. And the 'old boy's network' operates in this field as in many others – your contact may be doing a friend a favour rather than you.

Personal contact

You are quite likely to come across consultants at conferences or courses – they are major opportunities for them to market themselves. You will then see them in action and get some idea of what is on offer. Moreover, if you pursue the matter, you can hold at least a preliminary discussion about the possibility of their being able to provide help. However, you should be aware that someone who makes an effective presentation will not necessarily be a good consultant. But it is reasonable to assume that if a consultant has something to say and says it well then he or she is likely to have something worthwhile to contribute.

Published material

Published material in the form of a book or an article by an academic or a management consultant may reveal someone who is knowledgeable about an area of interest to you and who may be able to contribute to a project.

Registers

The most appropriate register is the one run by the IPM who will supply you two or three names in response to a request for help on a specific project. Consultants can only join the register on production of three satisfactory references, and to continue on it they are required to supply an extra reference each year. You can therefore be sure that the names submitted to you will be those of experienced consultants who are members of the IPM. In the four years since its establishment in 1990, well over 300 assignments have been handled, many for blue-chip and public sector organisations. The register at present consists of more than 200 consultants.

The MCIS, which is run in association with the Confederation of British Industry, maintains files on consultancy firms and individuals across a wide range of disciplines and in all parts of the country. All consultants on their register have to provide client references. Their stated aim is to undertake detailed research to match the specific requirements of those seeking advice or help with the skills and experience of each consultant.

Making a choice

Your choice of consultant will, of course, depend entirely on the nature of your organisation, the type of project, your own feelings and prejudices and those of your boss and your colleagues. The best course is to measure the available choices very carefully against the objectives of the project and the circumstances of your organisation.

If you do not have a specific consultant it is best to identify possible candidates and obtain comments about them from friends or colleagues if they are not well known or familiar to you, or else contact the IPM or MCIS register. You may then be able to narrow the field down to three or four (no more or you will waste too much time) and proceed to preparing the ground for selection.

6

Preparing the Ground

The success of a consultancy project depends to a considerable degree on the care with which you have prepared the ground. If your objectives for the work are unclear, not sufficiently thought through or not clearly stated, the consultant will be left to decide what is really needed. Because his or her understanding of the situation will be limited, the outcome could be incomplete. Alternatively, the consultant may try to avoid missing anything that might possibly have any bearing on the problem and attempt to cover every possible angle. The result will be a mass of data which it is impossible to interpret. A consultancy project is easily subject to information overload. Some consultants have been known to spend so much time collecting data that they find it impossible to reach logical and clear conclusions. In the process of doing this they can clock up a great deal of extra time and unnecessarily increase the costs of the assignment.

To avoid these problems it is essential to prepare the ground carefully by following the preliminary steps to identify the need as described in Chapter 4. By this stage you should have set objectives, drawn up a possible programme of work, estimated likely costs, cleared the project with higher authority if necessary, and assessed the likely reactions of managers, other employees and employee representatives. You should have identified possible external consultants, as described in Chapter 5.

The steps you now need to take to prepare for the project are as follows:

1. reaffirm the objectives of the assignment, taking into account the comments of colleagues and the reactions of managers, other employees and trade unions;
2. consider how you are going to use the consultants;
3. identify any other factors which are likely to affect the terms of reference and the conduct of the assignment;
4. produce preliminary terms of reference, which may be

modified after discussions with the consultants;
5. draft background notes to the project for use in briefing the consultants and a project team as appropriate.

Objectives

As mentioned in Chapter 4, a good way to start defining objectives is to produce a decision statement. For example you might say: 'We want to decide how best to develop an equitable and competitive pay structure which will enable us to attract, retain and motivate the quality of staff we require and ensure that we can manage relativities fairly and consistently.'

It is also useful when formulating objectives to establish the decision criteria which will help in drawing up terms of reference and can be used to measure the success of the assignment. For example:

- A fair and consistent method should exist for measuring relative job values.
- The job evaluation process we adopt should minimise the likelihood of our contravening equal pay for work of equal value legislation.
- The process used to measure relative job values should take into account the need for role flexibility.
- Market rate comparisons should be based on well-matched jobs and up-to-date information.
- The pay structure should provide for effective control without inhibiting necessary flexibility.
- The process for progressing pay within the structure should be based on the use of consistent and fair methods of assessing contribution and competence.
- The philosophy underpinning the pay structure and the basis upon which it operates should be fully understood and accepted by all levels of employees.
- The reward management processes used by the organisation should fit and support its culture, values and management style.

How the consultants will be used

How the consultants will be used obviously depends on the nature of the project or problem and the degree to which you or your colleagues already have experience and expertise in the areas concerned. The extent to which you will need their help will also depend on the resources you can provide – your own time and expertise and the time and expertise available elsewhere in the organisation, including the existence of internal consultants.

Another factor will be the amount of relevant data already available. Data collection can often be one of the most time consuming and expensive ways of using consultants – they should not be there simply to amass pieces of paper. You should do as much as possible yourself. For example, in a job-evaluation assignment you may have comprehensive job descriptions for all the jobs to be covered by the exercise. They may need to be expanded for analytical purposes but at least the ground work will already have been done. Even if you are not completely aware at this stage of the information the consultants are likely to need, you should be prepared to allocate resources to collect any routine data they wish to acquire.

You should also consider the extent to which you will have the internal resources required to implement the consultant's proposals. For example, many assignments, such as those concerned with performance management, may include a heavy training element. To what extent will you be able to undertake this with your own training resources, and how much expert help are you likely to need in preparing training material?

One of the factors to be taken into account in deciding on the involvement of your own staff, your colleagues and members of a project team, including both managers and employee representatives, is that they are more likely to 'own', the outcome of the assignment if they have taken part in developing recommendations.

As discussed in Chapter 3 there are many ways in which you can use consultants, depending on the project, the type of advice you need and the availability of internal resources. The options can be summarised as follows:

- giving mainly conceptual advice designed to provide stimulus and ideas for further development within the organisation;
- facilitating on a continuing basis an internal project team: providing ideas, training team members in analytical and other techniques and making suggestions on methods of proceeding for them to develop and implement;
- assisting you or a project team in the analytical and diagnostic stages of a project, discussing and agreeing recommendations but leaving the implementation to you;
- carrying out much or all of the analytical and diagnostic work and submitting recommendations for you to approve and implement;
- carrying out the whole process of analysis, diagnosis and formulating recommendations for agreement and becoming involved to a greater or lesser extent in implementation.

Other factors

Other factors you should take into account include the degree to which you will receive management support, the existence of internal politics, and employee and trade union attitudes.

Management support

You need to be as clear as possible about the degree to which your boss, the board and managerial colleagues are enthusiastic about or at least receptive to the project and the use of external consultants. You need to know how much support or opposition there may be from different quarters. This will enable you to steer the project and, as necessary, guide the consultants in how to avoid pitfalls. It could be argued that good consultants should be perceptive enough to identify problem people themselves. But it would be a pity to set up an assignment on the assumption that there is universal support and leave the consultant to find out at a later stage – possibly too late – that this is not the case. In any case, if you think that there will be opposition or indifference, you need to select a consultant who is likely to have the interpersonal skills and experience to cope with it.

Internal politics

There may be no outright opposition to a consultancy project but there could be people in the organisation who will play internal politics in an attempt to gain some advantage from it themselves, or even to prevent other people from gaining an advantage. Such hidden agendas sometimes emerge during a consultancy project and you should make yourself aware of the possibility.

You should be conscious of the potential disruptive power of internal politics. This may not be easy – the very nature of organisational politics means that it tends to work under the surface. But if you are acting as a sponsor for change – and when you initiate a consultancy project, that is what you are doing – you must take pains to make yourself aware of the possible effects of politics on the project. Sensitivity to this type of cultural issue is one of the key qualities that HR specialists within the organisation as well as outside consultants should possess.

Employee and trade union attitudes

You should try to establish the likely attitudes of employees and trade union representatives to any project which may affect their interests. You will need to take account of these in briefing employees, developing proposals and forming project teams. Wherever possible it is advisable to involve employee representatives in the project as members of a team, or at least to consult them on key issues. Awareness of attitudes and likely reactions will be important in preparing recommendations and managing the change process.

Terms of reference

The project's terms of reference are the guidelines for the consultants and everyone else involved in the project on what is to be achieved. The headings of a terms of reference statement will provide a basis both for briefing consultants and communicating details of the project to employees, and for programming the assignment and monitoring progress. They can be derived from the objectives and decision criteria. The following is an example of a terms-of-reference statement for a job-evaluation/pay-structure assignment:

- to develop a points-factor evaluation scheme;
- to use the scheme to evaluate all managerial, professional technical, supervisory and office jobs;
- to survey market rates;
- to develop a pay structure;
- to devise a system of progressing pay within the structure;
- to prepare procedures for administering pay and maintaining the structure;
- to communicate details of the structure and reward management processes to managers and staff;
- to provide training as required in assessing and rating performance and competence.

In this example, details of such aspects of the process as the job-evaluation system, the pay structure or the method of progressing pay are not given. The purpose of the assignment would be to develop approaches in each of these areas as well as the others specified in the terms of reference. But, there may also be occasions when you are certain of what you want done and would specify your requirements accordingly.

Terms of reference need not always be as elaborate as the example given above, but they should always spell out as precisely as possible what the consultant will be expected to do. For a recruitment assignment they could be:

- to prepare a job description and person specification for the position of . . .;
- to advise on the pay and benefits package;
- to prepare recommendations on a media plan budget and the text of advertisements and, subject to approval, to place advertisements;
- to sift applications;
- to interview applicants in order to produce a shortlist of six to eight candidates to be interviewed by . . ., which should be supported by full reports on each candidate;
- to take up references as required.

This example spells out exactly what the consultant is expected to do, but they may be modified following discussions with consultants, who will want to know precisely what you expect and may well make suggestions for changes based on their experience and understanding of your requirements.

If appropriate, you may also indicate in your terms of reference that the consultant will be working in conjunction with members of your staff or a project team who will be carrying out some of the tasks involved in the assignment. It is usually best not to be too specific about the nature and extent of these tasks; they can be left for discussion with the consultant.

Examples of terms of reference for a variety of situations are given in Appendix A.

Background information

It is useful to prepare some background information for briefing purposes. For a major project, where there may be a number of complex issues, a fairly detailed statement such as the example below for a job-evaluation/pay-structure assignment could be prepared. There is also an example of a simpler background statement for a recruitment assignment.

Example of background notes for a job-evaluation/pay-structure assignment

The size and complexity of the organisation has been increasing rapidly in recent years. There have been significant changes in a number of roles and a much more flexible team-working approach has been adopted in many key areas of the organisation's activities.

A salary structure exists for all the organisation's managerial, professional, technical supervisory and office staff – 2,500 in all. Directors are excluded. There is a separate pay structure for manual workers, who will not be covered by this exercise – although account should be taken of the possibility of developing an integrated reward structure in the future. This, however, is unlikely to take place for several years and it is meanwhile essential that we put our house in order so far as our staff salary structure is concerned.

The main features of the salary system are as follows:

- The structure covers rates of pay from £10,000 to £42,000 a year.
- There are 12 grades and the salary range for each grade extends to approximately 20 per cent above the minimum for the grade.
- The differential between grades is 12 per cent and grades overlap by an average of approximately 40 per cent.
- Jobs were initially graded following a ranking job-evaluation exercise. A process of whole-job comparisons is used to grade new jobs or regrade existing jobs.
- Pay progression through grades proceeds by eight fixed increments. The average increment is 2.5 per cent of the previous salary.
- There is scope for additional increments or half-increments if performance is rated A or B respectively on a five-point scale in the annual merit rating.
- Individual pay increases are carefully controlled by the personnel function.
- General increases are related to rises in the cost of living.
- Market-rate anomalies are 'red-circled', ie recognised as special cases.

It has become apparent that the system is failing to attract, retain and motivate the quality of staff the organisation needs. It is also evident that the problems of maintaining control over key parts of the system, such as grading and merit rating, are increasing. Dissatisfaction about a number of aspects of the system has been expressed by managers as well as staff, and the organisation is facing a claim under the Equal Pay Act.

Example of a background statement for a recruitment assignment

The organisation wishes to fill the newly created position of Market Development Manager. There have recently been a number of movements towards project and market diversification but a marketing strategy has now been formulated which is based on integrating these efforts under the control of a senior manager.

The department for which this manager will be responsible

will be entirely devoted to innovation in terms of new products and new markets for those products. Details of the products for development are given in the attached document [not included in this example], and it is envisaged that marketing effort will be concentrated in the European Community.

The Market Development Manager will take over existing developments and the team of three marketing executives responsible for them. He or she will be expected to formulate and carry out plans for implementing the development strategy and will also be expected to contribute to the reformulation of that strategy as necessary. Extra staff may need to be acquired.

The Market Development Manager will be responsible for all product-development and product-launch activities with the help as required of the existing Market Research Department. Market development may take the form of setting up new agencies overseas and creating new sales territories under appropriate management.

Should a new product or product range be developed which can stand alone as a profit centre this may be created as a separate division controlled by another marketing manager or possibly by the Market Development Manager.

7

Selecting Consultants

The selection procedure may include the following stages:

1. preparing a shortlist of consultants;
2. briefing the consultants in writing;
3. the consultant conducting a preliminary survey (only in more complex projects);
4. obtaining and reviewing proposals;
5. eliminating any consultants whose proposals are unacceptable and either asking the final shortlist to make formal presentations or interviewing them;
6. making the final choice.

This procedure may be simplified for a straightforward assignment or when you are clear about the consultant you wish to engage. It is, however, still essential to brief the consultants in such cases and you should obtain a proposal from them for discussion before agreeing the final terms of reference and programme.

Some organisations ask consultants to prepare proposals on the basis of a written brief only. Understandably, however, most consultants prefer to meet their prospective clients before submitting the proposal, in order to amplify the brief and obtain a better 'flavour' of the organisation and its requirements. Such preliminary meetings take time, but they do give you the chance to form some preliminary views about the consultants.

You will also have to decide whether to ask the consultants to make a formal presentation followed by an interview or discussion, or simply to interview them. A formal presentation means that you and anyone else involved in the selection has the opportunity to see the consultants in action (and the ability to make an effective presentation is almost certainly one of the skills which they will have to use). It also enables you to make fairly exact comparisons between the merits of the different consultants.

However, if the ability to make presentations is not a major consideration, interviews, especially if they are properly structured, can provide you with all the information you need.

You also need to decide at this stage who needs to be involved in the selection process. You may do it yourself, possibly in conjunction with one or two colleagues, especially anyone who will be involved in the project. If you are going to use a project team you could assemble its members in advance and involve them in the selection. The considerations to be taken into account in setting up a project team are discussed in the next chapter. If the project is a highly significant one with organisation-wide implications, there is much to be said for involving the chief executive or a board committee in the selection, possibly by meeting the consultants you prefer in order to give their final approval.

It is highly desirable to involve people who are going to work closely with the consultants in the selection process, if only to ensure that they will be able to work reasonably well together.

Preparing a shortlist of consultants

The first step is to identify consultants who are likely to meet your requirements in terms of their expertise, experience, resources, compatibility with your organisation's culture and ability to work well with you and your colleagues. The last two points may be difficult to establish with any certainty at the selection stage, but they should still be considered.

You may produce a shortlist of only one if you are confident from personal experience that you know a consultant who exactly fits your requirements – someone with whom you have worked before and who knows your organisation well. Even so, if the project is different from the work the consultant has previously carried out, it may be advisable to approach one or two other firms or individuals for purposes of comparison. Do not rely solely on recommendations, however enthusiastic they may be. You have to form your own judgement and this is best exercised by making your own selection (which could include the recommended firm) and comparing their proposals and presentations. Unless you are absolutely certain that someone will fit your requirements, it is always advisable to select from a number of firms or individuals.

On the other hand, you should not overdo it. You will waste a lot of your own time, never mind that of the consultants, if you invite too many tenders. I have known as many as 21 consultants competing for the same job (for a Middle Eastern government), each one of whom presumably produced a detailed proposal. One wonders how the final choice was made.

Consultants may not be inclined to take too much trouble over a proposal – or even bother to submit one – it it appears that the outcome is likely to be something of a lottery and they are not desperate for the work. So you might lose the chance to find the best firm or individual. If you restrict the number of firms or individuals you invite to tender to three or four, and tell them that is what you are doing you are likely to benefit from the greater incentive this gives the consultants to produce a really comprehensive proposal.

There is no optimum number for a shortlist, however. It depends how precise you can be about your requirements and the extent to which you can be sure you have narrowed down your choice to firms or individuals who are likely to meet them. My own practice has been to invite three or four tenders when I have no personal knowledge of the firms, and this has always given me a reasonable choice. When the job is fairly straightforward (eg recruitment or training delivery) and I know the firms, I have restricted my choice to two. On many occasions I have asked only one firm I know well to produce a proposal and have never regretted it.

A further reason for restricting the number of firms you invite to tender for a highly complex assignment is that you might otherwise spend too much time in the briefing process. Furthermore, if it is felt that a prior survey by the consultants is necessary, you will want to minimise the disruption by limiting the number to no more than three.

If consultants know that they are tendering for the job against competition – and they will usually ask if this is the case – they will want to know how many other firms are competing. But you do not have to tell them, and you certainly do not have to reveal their names at this stage.

If you ask three or four firms to submit proposals it will be interesting to compare their understanding of the requirements, their suggestions for carrying out the work and their estimates of

USING THE HR CONSULTANT

time and costs. A hidden advantage of this process of comparing and contrasting is that you can pick up ideas from all the proposals and store them away in your mind for use in setting up and managing the project. Bear it in mind, though, that consultants are, of course, aware that this happens and will try to tread the fine line between conveying to their client the fact that they know how to tackle the problem and providing free consultancy advice. Douglas Gray has advised consultants that:

> If your proposal has been rejected you may have provided too much information to your client who in turn uses the information for his or her benefit. In other words, you give away free consulting . . . You should be aware of the various ways that clients can innocently or intentionally obtain your advice for free.[4]

Inviting proposals

Having drawn up your shortlist, the next step is to get in touch with the firm or individual, asking if they would like to be considered. Alternatively, you may be approached directly by the consultant if he or she has been contacted by the IPM register of consultants or any other register.

When you issue your invitation you should indicate how they will be briefed if they accept – orally, in writing or both – and, in the case of a complex assignment, you may inform them that they will be given the opportunity of carrying out a preliminary survey before preparing their proposal.

Briefing consultants

The next step is to brief the consultants. As indicated above, this briefing may be oral with supporting documentation or, especially in larger or more complex assignments, in writing with perhaps a subsequent meeting. If you are asking a number of consultants to tender there is much to be said for a written brief, as it means that they all start from the same base and enables fairer comparisons to be made between their proposals. But the proposals will always be better – more perceptive and relevant – if you give the

64

consultants an opportunity to meet you and discuss the brief. This will also give you a preliminary opportunity to assess their quality, including their ability to ask searching questions. The considerations to be taken into account in preparing different types of brief are given below.

Briefing for a recruitment assignment

The brief for a recruitment assignment could be fairly simple. It would state the services required – advertising, sifting, short-listing, 'head-hunting' etc – and would include a preliminary job description and person specification, although good recruitment and executive search consultants will want to go through these carefully and will provide comments and suggest changes where they think the description or specification is incomplete or misleading and can be improved. The job description should be supported by an organisational chart and there should be an explanation of the reasons for the appointment. Again, good consultants will probe to ensure that they fully understand the reasons. They may ask why the previous job holder left, or why a new job has been created, or why there is no one available to fill the job from within if you are looking to recruit from outside the organisation.

The brief should incorporate information about any special features of the organisation which the consultant needs to take into account. Again good consultants, especially executive search consultants, will probe to ensure that they get the full picture. They will want to know about the culture of the organisation – its values and norms, its critical success factors, especially in the area for which the person to be appointed will be responsible, and any other information they can obtain which will enable them to achieve a good fit between the candidate and the organisation.

The brief may also include details of the proposed salary and benefits package. However, one of the advantages of using recruitment consultants is that you can obtain their recommendations on what would be a competitive salary.

Finally, you could provide information for the consultant to use in preparing advertisements and approaching and briefing candidates. This information might include annual reports, publicity material, a mission statement, details of products or services and future plans, if they can be revealed.

Briefing for training assignments

Training assignments may range from the delivery of training sessions in an established programme to conducting a full training needs analysis and the preparation and delivery of comprehensive training programmes..In more complex projects the briefing procedures outlined in the next section should be followed. If, however, it is simply a matter of delivering training sessions or facilitating a workshop in an established training programme, then less elaborate briefing material may be called for.

This sort of brief should incorporate a statement of the training need, an indication of how the proposed training input would help to meet that need, a description of how the input would fit into an existing training programme or course, together with details of the programme and a definition of the particular contribution the consultant would be required to make. This should indicate not only the content and duration of the input but also the preferred method – presentation, discussion, project work, case studies, simulations etc.

The briefing material would also include background information on the organisation, as for a recruitment assignment.

Larger-scale assignments

A larger-scale assignment is one which is concerned with a broader issue, related to organisational structures or processes, or HR processes and systems such as reward management, performance management, competence analysis, the design and operation of assessment centres, the design of computerised personnel information systems or a review of the organisation and activities of the HR function. The project is likely to involve the whole organisation or a major function or department within it. These are the sorts of assignment for which a more comprehensive and structured brief may be required under the headings of background, objectives, terms of reference and methods of working.

The briefing notes should also indicate how the selection procedure will be carried out. In a particularly complex assignment you may want to invite the consultant to carry out a preliminary survey.

Background As mentioned in Chapter 6, this statement describes the current situation and the nature of the need or problem which has made a consultancy project necessary. You may want to provide some indication of what you believe to be the causes of the problem but you need not go into too much detail. Problem diagnosis may be the main reason why you want to engage consultants and there may be situations when it is best not to offer an explanation at all – you may want to hear the consultant's opinions and compare them with any conclusions you yourself have reached. This will provide some indication of the perspicacity of the consultants and their ability to be creative in their analysis and diagnosis of a problem. In any case, you might not want to pre-empt their views.

If the project is about developing or introducing a new process, structure or system you will need to explain why you think this is necessary and to indicate broadly what you are seeking – for example, a pay structure, a new method of assessing performance, or new approaches to the continuous development of key employees. But you should not spell out exactly what you are proposing or any programme of work you envisage unless you are simply engaging the consultant as an 'extra pair of hands'. You will want to listen to or read the consultants' proposals on what they think should be done, again comparing them with your own ideas. If the consultants are any good they should be capable of being creative about the approach to be used and their ideas might not only complement your initial thoughts but also enhance them. This, after all, is probably one of the main reasons for engaging consultants and you should therefore give them every opportunity to be creative and yourself every chance to assess their creativity.

At this stage you might not want to reveal any potential problems in connection with the assignment such as management opposition or indifference, political manoeuvrings, hidden agendas or hostility from staff or trade unions. These are matters upon which you would want to brief the consultants at the start of the assignment itself, but there is probably no point at this stage in revealing, publicly and in advance, problems which might not materialise. Good consultants will, in any case, probe to establish if such problems exist, and their determination to do so will provide you with some indication of their effectiveness in unravelling problems.

Some people do not even reveal their own hidden agendas at the briefing stage, but this, I think, is undesirable. It may not be unreasonable to keep back your suspicions about potential difficulties elsewhere in the organisation, as these may not emerge as real problems during the course of the assignment. It is quite another matter deliberately to deceive a consultant by keeping back any part of the rationale for the project. If you do, the assignment will begin on a false basis, which could prejudice its later success. It must be founded on an open and trusting relationship between you and the consultant.

Objectives   In this section of the brief you should describe the aims of the project and the benefits you intend it to achieve (see Chapter 4).

Terms of reference   These set out the main tasks to be carried out as in the examples given in Chapter 6. It is not always necessary to spell out the terms of reference in detail in the briefing, as they may only emerge in their final form after discussion with the consultants. It may be advantageous to let the consultants produce their own ideas – this is another way in which you can test their competence.

The terms of reference should form the basis for developing a programme of work and each item can be used to check progress towards achieving the objectives of the assignment. They should also indicate the scope of the assignment and any limits within which the consultants will work. For example, the terms of reference for a job-evaluation assignment might state that the consultants will be expected to develop a tailor-made system of job evaluation to be applied to all staff excluding directors and manual workers.

It may also be desirable to tell the consultants whether they will be working with a project team or internal consultants, although you need not indicate at this stage exactly how this will happen. Such arrangements can be discussed during the initial meetings and when planning the project in detail.

Briefing on the selection procedure The briefing should include a description of the selection procdure, for example:

- a preliminary meeting;
- the submission of a written proposal;
- a final presentation and interview.

Surveys

In a highly complex assignment you might decide that the consultants should be given the opportunity to conduct an initial survey. Alternatively, after a preliminary briefing, they might themselves ask to be allowed to conduct one before preparing their proposal.

A survey involves the consultant obtaining more data about the project, possibly meeting a number of the people concerned. It is only necessary when it is impossible to convey enough information in a brief to enable a satisfactory proposal to be prepared. A survey can last half a day or several days; it obviously depends on the scale and complexity of the project. In very large projects it can involve a considerable amount of fact gathering and analysis, leading to a highly detailed proposal which may include diagnoses of the problems. Some consultants will want to charge for extensive surveys.

It is a matter of judgement whether or not you decide on or agree to a survey and whether you agree to pay for it. But it is essential that there should be a formal agreement before it is carried out, setting out its nature and objectives, the work to be carried out, how the results will be fed back to you and any charges involved.

Proposals

A proposal is the key document which a consultant produces in response to a brief. In a straightforward recruitment or training assignment it might be a simple letter stating what he or she undertakes to do and the costs involved.

A more elaborate proposal in response to a complex brief might consist of nine parts, as follows:

1. *Introduction.* This simply states that the proposal is about how the consultants could assist with the project and the headings under which the proposal is set out.
2. *Understanding of the need.* This section sets out how they see the need – the process or system to be developed or the problem to be solved. If they have had an opportunity to discuss the brief with you the proposal should not only reflect your own words but also provide additional comments to demonstrate that they are capable of and experienced in understanding the fundamental issues surrounding this type of project. They may refer to their experience of addressing similar problems or needs.

   They may rephrase your objectives for the project as stated in your brief to emphasise the specific and measurable outcomes which your discussions have highlighted. These could become reference points for measuring the progress and success of the assignment.
3. *Terms of reference.* They might simply restate the terms of reference for the record, bearing in mind that if the proposal is accepted, it will form part of the contractual basis for the assignment.

   They may, however, amend or enlarge on the terms of reference if they feel that this is necessary in the light of their understanding of the need. For example, a proposal from consultants in response to a job-evaluation/pay-structure brief as described earlier in this chapter could include in their 'understanding the need' section a suggestion that it would be important to establish the attitudes of employees to the existing pay system as a basis for developing new processes. The terms of reference might then include a proposal that they should conduct an attitude survey on your behalf.

   You do not have to accept their amendments, but they will be worth noting and it is always interesting to compare how different consultants respond to the given terms of reference. If you are looking for consultants who are capable of original, even lateral, thinking, this is one way of testing them.

4. *Approach*. This section will describe how they intend to carry out the project. They may want to describe their typical ways of working – eg that they prefer to work in close partnership with their clients in what is sometimes called collaborative consulting. They could also mention how they have tackled similar assignments.

They will aim to provide sufficient information to demonstrate their competence but, if they follow the advice of Douglas Gray, they will not provide enough information 'about their processes and techniques to provide a formula for the client to perform without the consultant'.[5]

5. *Project schedule*. This section schedules the specific tasks the consultants believe are required to meet the terms of reference. The timing and sequence of the successive stages should be indicated and this may usefully be accompanied by a bar chart or a functional flow chart. There should be an estimate of the total time needed for the assignment. The consultants should also state the points at which project reviews (milestone meetings) could be held.

The programme of work should break the assignment down into a progressive sequence of stages and an indication should be given of the work that will be completed (the deliverables) at the end of each stage. This process of staging the programme could be used as a basis for a later agreement that the consultants should complete the programme up to a certain stage (eg implementation), and that a decision be made later as to whether or not they should continue. This is a way of not over-committing yourself in advance.

You will need to examine this project schedule very carefully to assess the degree to which it is logical, comprehensive and realistic.

6. *Staffing*. In this section the consultants will indicate who will carry out each aspect of the work and who on their side will supervise the assignment. They should indicate whether this person or someone else will be the main contact with you in such aspects of the project as initiation, progress reviews and the discussion of recommendations.

If they propose to subcontract any part of the work to a specialist firm or a computer bureau, this should be indicated in this section, together with a statement of why it is thought to be necessary.

It should be stated what relevant experience of the consultants who would be assigned to the project have, and it is normal to attach their CVs to the proposal.

7. *Fees and costs.* This section should give the hourly or daily fee rates for each of the consultants who will be assigned to the project. An indication should be given of the number of hours or days it is proposed they should spend on the assignment. You should expect their time to be scheduled against each stage so that you obtain a clear picture of how the consultants propose to allocate their resources. They may suggest a range of time for each activity because of uncertainty about the internal resources available or some other factor.

The total estimated fees should be given on the basis of the hourly or daily rates and the estimated project time, and the proposal should indicate that travelling and subsistence expenses will be charged at cost. If there is likely to be some significant additional expenses, such as substantial travelling or computer bureau charges, the costs should be estimated. If it is a UK project and the consultant is registered for VAT the proposal will state that VAT at the normal rate will be charged on both fees and expenses. Any additional costs arising from sub-contracting work should also be specified.

The consultants may also break the costs down into stages, which can provide a useful basis for budgeting and controlling expenditure stage by stage. They may indicate which stages they believe to be essential to their submission and which are, as it were, optional extras – for example, help with implementation. This could provide you with some choice in your spending.

They may also give a range of costs for part or all of the assignment, if some aspects of the assignment have still to be confirmed, or for some other reason.

8. *Conclusion.* The concluding section may comprise comments about the likely benefits arising from the project and the consultants' interest in and competence to carry out the assignment.

9. *Appendices.* The appendices may include CVs, details of the firm, particulars of relevant experience and a statement of the consultants' standard terms and conditions.

The formats used by different consultants for their proposals may differ from this example, as each firm generally has its own style for proposals, but they will usually cover the same ground. However, if you want to make comparisons between a number of proposals easier you can request the consultants to follow a standard format.

Presentations

Large organisations and civil service departments usually request a formal presentation by the consultant, especially when several people are involved in the selection procedure. It provides you with the opportunity to see how each consultant performs in public and then with the chance to supplement their proposals and display their presentational skills. But you should try not to be too swayed by slick presentations.

Interviews

Presentations are not an essential part of a selection procedure but a searching interview is.

You should start the meeting by asking the consultants to run through their proposal, providing emphasis where necessary and supplementing their comments and views. You should then question them about any aspects which you think require further explanation. The sort of questions you might ask (if they have not already been answered) include:

- On what basis have you allocated time to each activity?
- How do you prefer to work with your clients?
- Could you explain why you have included this extra item in your suggested terms of reference?
- Could you give us more details of how you propose to carry out this part of the assignment.
- Could you expand on the relevant experience possessed by your firm and the consultants you propose to assign to the project?
- Have your ever met any problems in dealing with this sort of project and if so, how did you overcome them?

73

- Could you explain more precisely the roles of the consultants you propose to assign?
- How do you propose to manage the assignment?
- What are your views on involving the client's staff in this type of project?
- How do you find people within organisations tend to react to this type of project and how would you anticipate or deal with negative reactions?
- What arrangements do you propose to make for monitoring and reviewing progress?
- How will you present your recommendations?
- Do you foresee any problems in implementing the recommendations which will emerge from this project?
- What is your approach to change management?
- When can you start and when can you complete?

You should then give the consultants an opportunity to put questions to you. They will want to explore the reasons for the project and discuss the background and proposed terms of reference. They may ask additional questions such as:

- What resources will you be able to allocate to the assignment?
- Do you have in mind a project team, and if so how will it be constituted and how will it operate?
- Who would be our contact within the organisation during the course of the assignment?
- To whom will we report?
- Is there to be a steering committee? If so, who will be on it?
- What sort of support have you for this project from top management, middle management, supervisors, employees and trade unions?
- Do you foresee any opposition to the project from any quarter?
- Is there a hidden agenda?
- Are there any other factors we have not yet discussed which are relevant at this stage?
- What is the next step?
- When would you want us to start and finish?

Making the choice

The following factors should be taken into account in making the choice:

- the consultants' understanding of the aims of the project;
- their grasp of the real issues;
- the relevance of the programme of work they propose;
- their approach and working methods as revealed by their proposal and presentation, the interview discussion and, if appropriate, how they conducted a survey;
- their experience of working with project teams if you intend to make such an arrangement;
- the thoroughness with which they have prepared their presentation;
- the relevance of the firm's experience and of the consultants to be assigned to the project;
- the previous achievements of the firm and the individual consultants;
- the strength of the team – you should check each individual's qualifications, professional memberships and the length and relevance of his or her experience (membership of the IPM or the Institute of Training and Development would be a distinct advantage, as would membership of the Institute of Management Consultants);
- the ability of the team to adapt to the culture and management style of the organisation;
- the project control systems proposed;
- the proposed method of reporting;
- the time scale;
- the costs.

If there is a selection panel, they might use an evaluation sheet along the following lines:

CRITERIA   EVALUATION

1. Appreciation of task
2. Working methods
3. Thoroughness of preparation

4. Relevance of firm's experience
   and achievements
5. Strength of team
6. Ability of team to fit the organisation
7. Project control systems
8. Reporting methods
9. Time scale
10. Cost

All these points are relevant, but you should pay particular attention to the consultants' understanding of the project, the relevance and interest of their proposals, the strength of the team and their collective experience, the relevant experience of the firm, their methods of working, the time scale and the cost. Cost should not be the major consideration, however, as long as the total is within your budget or can be justified in terms of the benefits of the project. Your main criteria for making your choice should be:

- Can they do the work and achieve the results required?
- Will they provide added value?
- Can my colleagues and I work with them?

Your final decision on which consultants to use, and indeed on carrying on with the assignment as planned, should be based on the answers to the following questions:

- What contribution will be made to the bottom line (however that is defined)?
- To what extent will this project improve performance, productivity or profitability?
- What will the impact of this project be on the organisation's culture, values and methods of working?
- What are the likely reactions of managers, supervisors, employees and trade unions?
- Can we implement the likely outcome of these proposals smoothly?
- What are the additional costs involved in their implementation?
- Will they fit the organisation's culture and management style and will we be able to work well together?

You should already have posed questions of this kind when contemplating setting up the project, but you will be in a better position to answer them after you have considered and discussed the consultants' proposals, and met the consultants. Now is your last chance before taking the plunge and setting out to engage the consultant of your choice as described in the next chapter.

8

Engaging Consultants

There are four things you need to do when engaging a consultant:

1. Take up references as necessary.
2. Study his or her standard terms and conditions.
3. Reach a final agreement on assignment arrangements, including fees.
4. Prepare an assignment contract.

References

If you know the consultant personally and well, or have received a strong recommendation, you will probably not need to obtain references. It may also be unnecessary to take up references for someone with a considerable reputation, but there may be occasions when you want to check on a particular consultant, even if the firm has a good reputation.

When you know little or nothing about the firm or individual except what they have told you, however, it is essential to take up at least two references. They should be asked to supply you with the names of two or three referees who are members of firms for whom they have recently conducted assignments. It is then best to telephone them and ask the following questions:

- What type of assignment did this firm or individual carry out for you?
- Were you generally satisfied with the outcome of the assignment?
- Did the consultant(s) meet all their terms of reference?
- Did they keep to their programme?
- Did they keep within the agreed time and cost constraints?
- Did they work well with you and your colleagues?
- Did they produce practical recommendations which you have been able to implement?

Consultants' terms and conditions

You should always ensure that consultants' terms and conditions are acceptable. Typical standard terms will incorporate the following information:

- the fact that the terms are related to a specific proposal;
- the arrangements for paying fees and expenses (eg monthly) and the requirement for invoices to be settled on receipt;
- a warning that fees may be increased as a result of inflation but that, in the event of an increase, due notice (eg three months) will be given;
- the basis on which the consultant's time will be charged (eg a daily or hourly rate), how travelling time or unavoidable weekend work will be charged for and a provision that there will be no charge when the consultant is absent through illness or on holiday;
- the basis on which normal travelling and subsistence expenses will be charged;
- the basis on which extraordinary expenses will be charged subject to the client's prior approval;
- a statement to the effect that, while the time and cost estimates were given in good faith on the basis of the survey and discussions, circumstances might arise which could not have been foreseen at the time, necessitating an extension to the time required and therefore an increase in costs, to be agreed in advance with the client.

It is to your advantage to have the arrangements for charging fees and expenses spelt out and it is understandable that consultants would want to cover themselves against inflation or unforeseen circumstances. You will have to decide, possibly with legal advice, whether any other terms presented to you are acceptable. If you feel that anything is unacceptable you will have to negotiate changes.

Reaching a final agreement

Before confirming the engagement you will obviously have to

79

agree on all the key aspects of the assignment. You can inform them that you are proposing to invite them to carry out the project subject to final agreement on certain specified aspects, the terms of engagement or the cost of fees.

The items you may want to discuss could include specific points about the consultants' terms and conditions. You could also run through your own standard letter of engagement or contract (see below) to explain its requirements and obtain agreement to its terms (or modify them if appropriate). The other items you might want to discuss are the consultants' fees, deliverables from the assignment, your contribution, the programme and timetable, reporting arrangements (progress and final), how they propose to manage the assignment, the precise role of each consultant, the setting up of a project team or working party and the provision of facilities by you.

Fees – basis of charging

It is quite common for consultants to quote a daily rate, although there may be situations when they feel that an hourly rate is more appropriate, perhaps when they are providing intermittent services or advice, or regularly working long hours. Consultants typically assume a seven-hour day, excluding lunch, when calculating an hourly rate, so their hourly rate would be one-seventh of their daily rate. They may want to round this up to take account of lack of continuity.

A daily rate suggests that if the consultants are working full time for you they will not charge more if they work for longer than your normal working hours, but they will usually expect – and you should expect them – to work your normal hours if they are providing continuous services. Even when they are visiting your establishment for a day's work away from their base you can reasonably expect them to travel mainly in their own time and arrive at your office or factory not much later than your normal starting time. On the other hand you may make allowances if they have to travel some distance from their base to one of your other establishments, and it would be quite reasonable for consultants to charge for the time travelling to and from you if they are engaged for only part of a day.

Negotiating fees

If you think the total cost of the assignment is too high you can always try to negotiate a lower fee rate or a lower total cost. As with all negotiations, if the consultants are not too concerned about winning the assignment they will be less likely to give way, but if they badly want the job they may be prepared either to reduce their rate or to discuss ways of reducing the time they spend on the assignment. Some consultants take the view that the rates they charge are what they are worth and will not negotiate a lower rate, although they may be prepared to discuss reducing their input as long as they do not believe that this would prejudice the success of the assignment.

Another approach you might adopt if you are concerned about costs escalating beyond your budget is to negotiate a fixed-price contract in return for agreed deliverables. The fixed price would, of course, be one within your budget and your could try to persuade the consultants to reduce their overall quotation to meet this figure.

You should always bear in mind that even the most professional and experienced consultants will sometimes find it difficult to produce an accurate estimate of the time required for complex assignments. In these circumstances, a detailed analysis of their input and the contribution your staff will make to the project may convince them that the objectives of the assignment could be achieved in less time.

If you do not want to overcommit yourself, you can discuss a staged approach which would mean that they would only be contracted to carry out certain parts of the work – up to the implementation stage, for example – and a decision on whether or not they should provide further assistance could be made during the course of the assignment.

Expenses

Consultants should charge the expenses which they have incurred 'wholly and necessarily as part of the project' at cost plus VAT if they are VAT rated.

Some clients expect their consultants to travel the same class as their own executives, which may mean standard class by rail or economy class by air. They might also expect them to charge the organisation's own mileage rate for travel by car. Some consultants, however, will expect to be reimbursed their travelling expenses in accordance with their own firm's standards, which could be first or business class, and at their own mileage rate. They would also expect to stay in good if not the most luxurious hotels.

If there is likely to be a lot of travel it is as well to agree on the basis for charging expenses before the assignment begins. You should bear in mind, however, that the extra cost of first- or business-class travel may be worth it if it means that the consultants are fresher and able to do a better job after a long journey.

It would be perfectly reasonable to request a schedule of travelling expenses and vouchers to back it up.

Deliverables

'Deliverables' is a term which has become increasingly used in consultancy circles – and rightly so. It emphasises that the consultants are there to deliver results, which are usually more specifically defined than in a terms of reference statement. A statement of deliverables indicates exactly what you will get and when. In a job-evaluation/pay-structure assignment, for example, the consultant may undertake to deliver to you by a certain date a full report on the degree to which your pay structure is competitive, based on an analysis of the information contained in published surveys and aiming to match, as far as possible, your benchmark jobs with the jobs included in the surveys.

The statement may specify the form which each of the deliverables is to take: a report, a presentation, a training course, a shortlist of six candidates, a job-evaluation scheme fully written up etc.

It is a useful exercise before starting an assignment to agree on a set of deliverables, thus focusing the terms of reference on specifics and timings. For example, the statement of deliverables for a performance-management assignment might read like this:

Deliverable	By	Format
1. Briefing to management on basic principles of performance management	Day 2	Presentation
2. Draft notification to employees of the proposal to introduce performance management and what it entails	Day 3	Memorandum
3. Proposals for discussion by project team on approach to performance management	Day 5	Memorandum/ presentation
4. Detailed description of performance-management scheme for discussion by project team.	Day 8	Memorandum/ presentation
5. Documentation on the process of performance management as agreed by project team	Day 10	Report
6. Plan for pilot test, co-ordination of the test and analysis of lessons learned for discussion by team	Day 15	Briefing, personal contact and report
7. Final version of documentation for agreement by project team	Day 18	Report
8. Briefing to management on the proposed process	Day 20	Presentation
9. Briefing notes for employees	Day 22	Memorandum
10. Training course programme and material	Day 27	Fully documented training programme
11. A team of company staff capable of conducting training	Day 40	Training course, conduct of pilot scheme courses in conjunction with the company's training staff
12. Evaluation of process	Day 40+ 12 months	Report

When drawing up a statement of deliverables it would be proper to establish in advance that some of them will be dependent on the contribution of the organisation's staff or may be affected by circumstances beyond the consultants' control.

Your contribution

You should agree with the consultants what you will contribute to the assignment at each stage in the shape of people to carry our fact-finding, information-processing and analytical work and to take part in training programmes and implementation.

Programme and timetable

It is advisable at this stage to run through the programme again to ensure that both parties are satisfied that it is realistic and achievable. The starting date and the estimated completion date should also be agreed.

Reporting arrangements

Broad agreement should be reached on what progress reports you would expect at 'milestone' meetings and who would make them. Similarly, the format of the final report should be agreed.

Project management

There must be agreement on who will be responsible for managing the assignment and how you and the consultants will work together. It may not be possible to be absolutely precise about this and the arrangements can differ considerably, depending on the nature of the assignment. For example, if the consultants were simply acting as an 'extra pair of hands' you would be the project manager. If, however, their remit were to conduct the whole assignment and you were not involved except at progress meetings and in reviewing interim and final proposals, then they would be the project managers. There are many variations between these two extremes. Most typically, projects are managed on a shared basis, with you taking the lead and the consultants managing the process.

Consultant roles

If a team of consultants is assigned to the project it is necessary to confirm at this stage who will be leading the consultancy team, which member of the team will be doing what and who your main day-to-day contact will be, if it is not the team leader.

Project team

If you have decided to set up a project team you should seek the consultants' views on its composition and terms of reference, especially if they have previous experience of working with project teams (and in these circumstances this would be one of your selection criteria).

Facilities

The consultant might want to discuss the facilities you will provide such as office space and administrative support.

The assignment contract

When you engage a consultant you are obviously forming a contractual relationship. An essential feature of a contract is an exchange of promises, expressed or implied, by the parties to do, or refrain from doing, certain specified acts, and it is enforceable by law.

Contracts can be oral or written, but the problem with an oral contract is that if the parties disagree, it is difficult to establish what the original agreement was. A written contract simply records what you have agreed, and can be quite informal. If a consultant writes to you confirming his or her agreement to your terms and the four essential elements of a contract are present, you have a simple informal contract. These four elements are:

1. *Offer.* If a consultant submits a proposal to you in writing that constitutes an offer.
2. *Acceptance.* This has to be clearly demonstrated, preferably by your accepting the consultant's proposal in writing.
3. *Consideration.* This takes the form of a promise to pay money or provide some other benefit in exchange for services rendered.
4. *Intention to create legal relations.* This is presumed in a commercial context.

The basic consultancy contract consists of:

- The written proposal, which describes what is to be done, how it is to be done, who will do it, the time scale (starting and finishing dates), fee rate and costs (it may be extended or amended by subsequent discussions and if so the agreed notes of the decisions made in these discussions should be attached as an annex to the proposal);
- the standard terms and conditions of the consultant, which should be attached to the proposal, with any agreed amendments noted;
- the client's acceptance of the proposal and the standard terms and conditions, which can be a fairly simple letter or a more elaborate form of contract as discussed below.

If you have any doubts about the nature of the contract and its terms you must obtain legal advice. The information given below is for illustrative purposes only, and cannot be relied upon to be legally watertight in all circumstances.

Acceptance letters

In its simplest form, and assuming that there have been no additions or amendments to the consultants' original proposal and terms and conditions, an acceptance letter could include words to the effect that you confirm the engagement of the consultants to carry out a specified assignment in accordance with their proposal. The letter might spell out the key elements of the contract such as the programme of work, the timing, the consultants to be assigned to the project, the fee rates and costs and acceptance of the consultants' standard terms and conditions as set out in the proposal. You would also confirm the starting date and any prior arrangements that need to be made.

More formal contracts

Your organisation may have a standard form of contract for consultants and other service providers, in which case you would follow its provisions. If not, and if you want a formal contract, the main points you may want to include are summarised below:

General

- date of agreement;
- identification of client and consultant.

Project arrangements

- brief description of the project (refer to briefing papers);
- scope and content of the assignment, including terms of reference, programme of work, deliverables and any other relevant data included in the briefing papers or finally agreed proposal;
- provision for changes in work arrangements;
- designation of individuals in client's and consultant's organisation responsible for policy decisions;
- date for starting and completing the assignment, including any staging arrangements.

Responsibilities of the consultant

- provision of a project leader, consultants and other services as specified in the proposal;
- availability for conferences with client;
- reporting arrangements (progress and final reports);
- safeguarding of information supplied by the client (a confidentiality clause).

Responsibility of the client

- information, services and facilities to be provided;

- availability for conferences with consultant;
- arrangements for reviewing and approving progress and final reports.

Duration and amendment of contract

- stipulation of completion date, either by stating a specific date or by indicating the duration of the operation from the execution of the contract;
- provision for the modification or amendment of the specified date or other items (eg work to be done or time required) in the contract by mutual agreement;
- provision for termination by either party.

Financial provisions

- fee rates and agreed costs;
- provision of proof for Inland Revenue purposes that the consultant is an independent contractor and can in no way be treated as an employee of the company (an important point if you are engaging a former employee as a consultant as the Inland Revenue will need to be convinced that the individual is no longer employed by you, thus making him or her liable for tax and NI contributions and your firm not liable for employer's NI contributions);
- timing of invoicing by the consultant and supporting documentation required, eg schedule of time spent and expenses;
- schedule of allowable expenses, which may specify the class of air or rail travel and car mileage allowance;
- arrangements for agreeing in advance any additional expenses;
- arrangements for agreeing on the use by the consultant of subcontractors, bureaux or agencies and for approving in advance the costs thereof.

9

Starting the Assignment

To get off to a good start and to ensure that the project runs smoothly you need to do seven things:

- decide who is going to exercise overall leadership of the project (probably yourself if you are the sponsor) and who is going to be responsible for project management (usually the consultants);
- decide whether or not any staff from within the organisation will take part alongside the consultants;
- confirm the programme;
- confirm the deliverables;
- discuss and agree methods of working with the consultants and arrangements for monitoring progress;
- as necessary, set up a steering group, project team, task force or working party;
- decide how employees should be informed about the assignment and be involved in the project.

Leading the assignment

If you have sponsored the project, defined its terms of reference, engaged the consultants and agreed the programme of work and deliverables then it is *your* project. You lead it and only you can be held accountable for the results. Good consultants understand this perfectly well, so you do not need to spell it out.

Leadership implies delegation and when entering into a contract with consultants you are delegating work to them. If they are carrying out a specific task for you then they are accountable to you for the effective performance of that task. If they are managing the whole assignment on your behalf then they are the project managers and you are the project leader.

This does not mean, of course, that consultants are there just to do what you say. They are engaged to use their expertise and independent judgement to deliver results in the form of recommendations which you accept in total, reject in total (which should never happen) or modify in some way (which frequently happens). During an assignment you should review progress from time to time, but you should not interfere unless the progress is unsatisfactory or something is clearly going wrong.

Staffing the assignment

Assuming that the project is not a straightforward recruitment or training delivery assignment, you will need to decide what staff, if any, you are going to provide from within the organisation to work with the consultants.

If people of the right quality are available there is everything to be said for involving them. They will not only provide extra resources for data collection and analytical work but will also be able to contribute on the basis of their intimate knowledge of the organisation. Furthermore, taking part in a consultancy project can provide valuable experience. You could discuss with the consultants the possibility of staff from within the organisation (including yourself) carrying out specific parts of the assignment. Alternatively, your staff could join the consultancy team as full or part-time members under the direction of the project manager.

Programme

The next thing to do is to confirm the programme of work. This will mean deciding what data needs to be collected in advance, what interviews or meetings should be set up and preparing a final timetable for the project. Much of this will probably have been set out in the consultants' proposal and discussed in subsequent meetings before engaging the consultants, as described in Chapter 8.

Data collection

The more data that can be collected before the start of the programme the better, and you should discuss what is required in advance with the consultants. Depending on the project, it could include information on such matters as organisational structures, mission statements, policy statements, definitions of departmental or functional responsibilities, job descriptions, pay structures, details of procedures for evaluating and grading jobs, performance appraisals, salary reviews, management development, career planning and employment matters generally. Where available, details should be obtained of existing business and human resource strategies and policies. In addition, if studies and reports already exist in the area under consideration, these should be made available to the consultants. The aim is to minimise the time they spend on relatively routine data collection.

Information gathering or discussion meetings

Consultancy projects almost inevitably mean meetings, including meetings to brief management and staff, to obtain information or discuss the issues and to obtain views on current practices, relevant problems and their likely causes and suggestions on what needs to be done. A phenomenon all consultants notice when they carry out such meetings is how many good ideas exist in the organisation which have never seen the light of day. One of the advantages of using external consultants is that, if they know their job, they can stimulate people to make suggestions which they might otherwise have kept to themselves. This is a sad commentary on the inability of many organisations to make full use of the contributions their employees are capable of making.

Meetings may have to be planned some time in advance and scheduled into the programme. It can be a tiresome business but it is necessary.

Timetable

At this stage a final and detailed programme should be prepared in discussion with the consultants and anyone else taking part in the project.

The most useful way of summarising the programme is a chart like the one in Figure 9.1. This divides the programme into the main activity areas and shows the starting and finishing time for

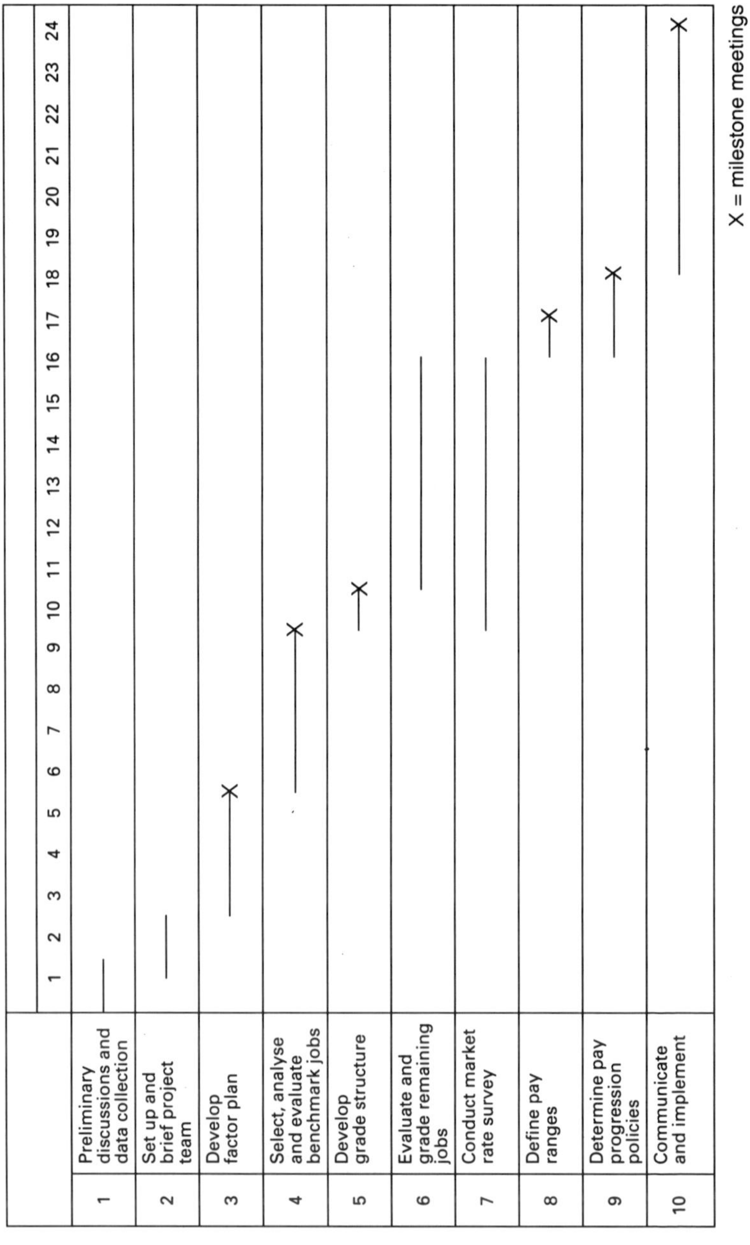

		1	2	3	4	5	6	7	8	9	10	11	12	13	14	15	16	17	18	19	20	21	22	23	24
1	Preliminary discussions and data collection																								
2	Set up and brief project team																								
3	Develop factor plan					X																			
4	Select, analyse and evaluate benchmark jobs									X															
5	Develop grade structure											X													
6	Evaluate and grade remaining jobs																								
7	Conduct market rate survey																								
8	Define pay ranges																	X								
9	Determine pay progression policies																			X						
10	Communicate and implement																								X

X = milestone meetings

Figure 9.1 *Job-evaluation/pay-structure assignment programme*

each activity. It also indicates where there is an overlap between activities, and the timing of progress or 'milestone' meetings can also be shown.

The programme should define not only what has to be done and when, but also who is to do it. This can sometimes be recorded on the chart but it is usually necessary to have a separate schedule dividing the responsibility between the consultants, members of the organisation's staff and the project team, if any. This schedule could be broken down to show the responsibilities of individual members of the consultants' or organisations' teams so that everyone taking part in the project knows exactly what is expected of him or her.

Deliverables

The deliverables should have been agreed at the proposal stage or in the discussions prior to engaging the consultants. They should now be confirmed and linked to the programme and schedules of responsibilities.

Methods of working

As overall project leader you should discuss with the consultants how you and your colleagues are going to work with them. You may emphasise at this stage that they are responsible for project management, but you should also discuss liaison arrangements, how your own staff and others from within the organisation will work with or, in some cases, for the consultants, and provisions for progress or 'milestone' meetings.

Progress meetings are best slotted into the programme at the end of each main stage, and they should be used to discuss the achievement of the agreed deliverables. Clearly, if anything is going badly wrong you should sort it out at the time, but these meetings provide opportunities to review and if necessary revise working arrangements, and to consider any underlying problems as they arise. They also serve as a forum for discussing interim findings and considering the emerging shape of the final recommendations.

Steering committees and project teams

Discussions should also take place with the consultants on your proposals, if any, for setting up a steering committee or project team. The consultants' role should be clarified.

Steering committees

In large and complex assignments which affect the interests of a number of directors or senior managers it may be felt that a steering committee should be set up to consider and agree interim and final recommendations. Steering committees are useful in giving people a sense of involvement but they may get in the way of the project if their members try to become *too* involved. It is often better not to set up a formal steering committee but simply to designate those directors or senior managers, including of course the chief executive, who will finally agree recommendations and the implementation programme. This could be done at a normal board meeting to which you report together with the consultants (if appropriate), or at a special *ad hoc* meeting. It may be desirable at the end of a particularly important project with a number of strategic implications to arrange a special meeting or conference of directors and senior managers at which you and the consultants present their findings and recommendations.

Project teams

Project teams (which may also be called task forces, working parties or work groups) can be a useful way of involving interested parties in the assignment. They can give the consultants the benefit of their collective views and experiences, discuss and comment on the consultants' findings and recommendations, take part in analytical work, make joint decisions on certain key aspects of the assignment (possibly subject to approval by higher authority), and represent interest groups within the organisation.

A project tream can help with implementation and in some activities such as job evaluation the team can be turned into a permanent panel, using the knowledge its members have gained during the development of the scheme to help in its administration. If there are employee representatives on the team they can keep their fellow employees informed and discuss any matters of principle with them.

A project team should normally have no more than six to eight members, representing a cross-section of managers and, preferably, employees. The leader of the team should be the sponsor of the project and the consultants should attend meetings and may help to facilitate them. The team should have terms of reference – eg 'to provide guidance, advice and assistance to the project manager and the project consultants and to discuss and agree recommendations arising from the project'. The programme of work for the project team should be co-ordinated with the assignment programme and their meetings should be scheduled to fit the main segments and review points of that programme.

The extent to which project teams are involved in assignments will vary. At one extreme the team may be totally responsible for the assignment and its members may carry out much of the work with the consultants servicing the team, carrying out specified analytical and diagnostic activities and feeding it with ideas. In this case the consultants would not lead the team but might still exert considerable influence over its deliberations. At the other extreme, the project team may simply act as a review and decision-making body. The consultants would attend team meetings but would be largely responsible for the assignment work.

Project teams can, however, present problems. They can become immersed in too much detail and may develop a life of their own, holding lengthy meeting with endless discussions without making any progress. They must be kept under control – their job is to make progress not to talk about it. There are situations where it is far better to let the consultants get on with the job. according to their remit, leaving you to control the project through progress meetings rather than bogging them down with a meandering project team.

Communicating with employees

If one exists, a project team with employee representatives can take responsibility for employee communications, but as we have seen, a project team is by no means an essential feature of an HR assignment.

If you do not have a project team, you should still take pains to keep employees informed of what is happening and consult both them and managers about issues about which they will be concerned. The implementation stage will be much easier if there have been good communications before and during the assignment and if employees have been involved in the project.

Managers and other employees should be thoroughly briefed at the start of an assignment on its objectives, how it will be conducted, the role of the project team if there is one, who will be taking part in the project and how its progress and findings will be communicated to them.

If this briefing is not done carefully those who feel they may be affected by the project may worry unnecesssarily, or may be unco-operative. The arrival of consultants in an organisation often causes alarm bells to ring. Sometimes this may be justified: a reorganisation, a business process re-engineering assignment or a cost-cutting exercise will almost certainly create fears about the future. You cannot and should not deny or disguise the fact that such assignments may result in reduced staffing levels or changes in responsibilities. You must be frank about what you are doing in the interests of the organisation, emphasising where possible that steps will be taken in consultation with employees to mitigate the impact of change if there is any danger of it being detrimental to their interests. These steps might include retraining, early retirement provisions, an undertaking to reduce numbers by natural wastage or outplacement advice and generous redundancy provisions.

Typical reactions to consultants are: that they are hatchet men or women, doing the organisation's dirty work for it; or that job-evaluation exercise is really a means of assessing staff and identifying poor performers; or that a performance–management system is simply an adjunct of the disciplinary procedure; or that quality circles are a threat to the authority and role of trade unions. I have come across all these reactions. I have received a deputation of senior managers who thought their performance was being assessed rather than their jobs evaluated; met staff representatives who thought a refined disciplinary procedure was being put in rather than a performance-appraisal system; and

been summoned to attend a mass meeting of the officials in the Republic of Ireland's Supreme and High Courts (registrars, bankruptcy commissioners etc – a formidable gathering) to explain how a layman could presume to evaluate the relative size of their highly legal and unique jobs.

To avoid or at least minimise such reactions you should take great care over pre-assignment communications. You will never entirely eliminate fears about some projects but you can certainly alleviate them.

Briefings about a forthcoming assignment should be prepared in written form but as far as possible they should be presented in person by you with the support of the consultants. Even if it is impossible or undesirable to address mass meetings of employees, you should always try to talk to key directors and managers and trade union or staff representatives.

10

Working Effectively with Consultants

If you have prepared for the assignment thoroughly, you should have a sound basis for working effectively with consultants. To build successfully on this foundation it is necessary to:

- understand how good consultants will aim to achieve a high-quality, added-value result, so that you can provide them with encouragement and support;
- establish criteria for measuring the consultants' performance;
- take steps to fulfil your part of the contract;
- monitor the progress of the assignment;
- be prepared to step in and take action if things appear to be going wrong;
- discuss interim findings and conclusions with the consultants so that you can work together to produce the optimum recommendation or solution;
- ensure at all times that the assignment is moving towards recommendations that can be implemented without undue disruption or cost and with the active consent of those concerned;
- communicate and consult regularly with all managers and other employees and employee representatives who have an interest in the outcome of the project.

Each of these requirements is discussed below.

How the best consultants conduct assignments

It is useful to know how the best consultants conduct assignments as this provides a yardstick against which you can measure how your consultants are performing. The areas to consider are fact finding and analysis, diagnosis, client relations, quality assurance and recommendation.

Fact finding and analysis

Fact finding and analysis can occupy as much as 60 per cent of consultants' engagement time and are the hub of all consultancy activities. Good consultants will emphasise the 'people' side of this process and a major firm of consultants (KPMG Peat Marwick McClintock) state in their golden rules of consultancy that 'the art of consultancy is 20 per cent technical, 80 per cent people'.

The consultants will want to establish the facts by interviewing, holding group meetings and sifting through documents. If they want to carry out in-depth interviews they may schedule no more than three or four a day. They will want not only to gather information and hear people's views but also to probe. Consultants often have to dig away to get the information they require, not because people are deliberately withholding information – although this can happen – but because they do not appreciate the significance of the information they possess. You may have to be prepared for managers and others to protest about the persistent and probing nature of a consultant's questions. Your answer should be that the consultant is paid to ask penetrating questions and to get answers to them. As long as he or she does this politely, managers have no cause for complaint.

Diagnosis

Analysis leads to diagnosis: the identification of the need or the causes of the problem. Much of the value which can be added by consultants lies in their expertise as diagnosticians. It is their job to find out what help their clients actually need and to define what should happen. The deviation between what is and what should be constitutes the need to be satisfied or the problem to be solved.

Good consultants study symptoms, but they penetrate beneath the surface to identify causes. Causal factors may sometimes be obvious, but they are more often hidden. Difficulties in identifying causes are particularly acute when the situation has been strongly influenced by the behaviour of the people involved, which is usually the case. Politics, power plays, conflict, demotivated executives or staff, poor-quality people and inadequate teamwork can all contribute to the creation of a problem.

As Arthur Turner has said:

> Competent diagnosis requires more than an examination of the external environment, the technology and economics of the business, and the behaviour of non-managerial members of the organisation. The consultant must also ask why executives made certain choices that now appear to be mistakes or ignored certain factors that now seem to be important.[6]

Good consultants will draw members of the organisation into a diagnostic process, both formally through working parties and project teams and informally through day-to-day contacts with people at all levels of the organisation. If they know their job, they will make great efforts to build and maintain such contacts, and they should not be discouraged from doing so as long as the contacts are to the purpose, ie testing hypotheses and assessing alternative courses of action.

Arthur Turner quotes a consultant as explaining:

> We usually insist that client team members are assigned to the project. They, not us, must do the detail work. We'll help, we'll push – but they'll do it. While this is going on, we talk with the CEO every day for an hour or two about the issues that are surfacing, and we meet with the chairman once a week. In this way, we diagnose strategic problems in connection with organizational issues. We get some sense of the skills of the key people – what they can do and how they work. When we emerge with strategic and organizational recommendations, they are usually well accepted because they have been thoroughly tested.[7]

Client relations

Good consultants pay a lot of attention to creating good relationships with their clients because they recognise that they need the co-operation of staff for fact finding, discussion of ideas, agreement and implementation. They know, however, that they cannot insist on co-operation, and cannot even expect it. However carefully the reasons for engaging consultants have been explained, there will usually be some resistance to them and sometimes a lot. As I said in the last chapter, consultants are resented for a wide variety of reasons, and this resentment needs to be anticipated when staff are briefed and when selecting consultants. You should consider in advance the extent to which it may emerge and engage consultants who will be able to manage it. The nature of HR consultancy means that maturity is a key requirement, although, of course, maturity is not necessarily an attribute of age.

A large consultancy firm has issued the following advice to its consultants on the pitfalls they may meet in dealing with clients:

- The sponsor may be different from the client.
- Day-to-day contacts may not be the 'client'.
- You are *always* on duty; never criticise the firm.
- Do not 'go native', even on very long assignments.
- Keep out of internal politics (but be aware of them).
- Avoid close relationships with client staff (but be aware of them).
- Keep confidences to yourself.
- Do not say things to please in the heat of the moment. Do not confuse being *liked* with being *respected*.

Quality assurance

A number of consultancies have met the BS5750 quality assurance standards with the aim of demonstrating to clients that they are committed to quality and are able to meet their quality needs. The fact that a consultancy firm has not qualified for these standards does not, however, mean that they are not interested in providing a quality service to their clients.

All large consultancies and many smaller ones have developed comprehensive control systems and procedures for project time and cost management which include computer support and the extensive filing of checklists, working papers and other documents. Projects may be controlled by obtaining sign-offs for deliverables although this can be mechanistic; as Ing says, 'How often does an assignment's thrust and direction change as the assignment proceeds, as the facts discovered during the assignment change the specification and perception of the problem?'[8] He recommends that there should be regular discussions of the priorities and nuances of the client's need: 'The assignment control parts of the quality system should not be inward looking but include mechanisms to track quality in the *eyes of the client.*'

Recommendations

Consultants will sometimes spend a good deal of time writing reports in which the information and analysis are clearly presented and the recommendations are convincingly related to the diagnosis upon which they are based. They believe their job has been done when they present a consistent and logical plan to improve the diagnosed situation. They recommend and the client decides whether and how to implement.

But as Arthur Turner says:

> This set-up is simplistic and unsatisfactory. Untold numbers of seemingly convincing reports, submitted at great expense, have no real impact because – due to the constraints outside the consultant's assumed bailiwick – the relationship stops at the formulation of theoretically sound recommendations that can't be implemented.[9]

The better consultants avoid this problem by continually testing their proposals with their clients to sound out their reactions. In a successful assignment the consultant continually strives to understand what actions, if recommended, are likely to be implemented and where people are likely to want to do things differently. Some consultants may be tempted to confine recommendations to those steps which they believe will be implemented easily, failing to recognise that it is their job to produce the optimum solution and to anticipate any implementation problems. They should not seek the easiest way, but they must nevertheless be realistic about what difficulties might arise and how they can be overcome.

This raises the question of whether you should expect consultants to recommend what they believe to be right or what they think will be acceptable. It can be argued that a consultant is bound to offer the 'best' solution, but what is the 'best' solution – the one the consultant believes in or the one the client can implement to good effect? As Douglas Gray has commented:

> What is theoretically best, as consultants see it (and how certain

102

can they be that they are right?) is not necessarily best in practice. To take an arrogant and rigid professional view is not likely to get a consultant far.[10]

What you can reasonably expect from consultants is that they will adopt a professional approach in making recommendations which they believe to be appropriate *and* practical in terms of the impact they will make and the likelihood of their being implemented. You should not be paying them for advice which is geared to pleasing you rather than meeting the real needs of the organisation. They – and you – must recognise that their recommendations will not always be easy to implement and will not please everyone. Consultancy projects produce change and it is unlikely that this can be managed with ease (approaches to managing change following consultancy recommendations are discussed in the next chapter).

Performance criteria

Your expectations of how the consultants should operate and what they should deliver can be based on the above criteria. There are, however, other factors to take into account, and the following checklists set out the main considerations.

Assignment checklist

You should satisfy yourself that the consultants have:

- carried out a thorough fact-collecting exercise without wasting time obtaining unnecessary information;
- produced an analysis of the facts affecting the need or problem which is convincing and accurate and demonstrates that they understand not only the facts but also the circumstances surrounding the facts, including the culture of the organisation;
- produced a diagnosis of the need or problem which follows logically from the analysis and addresses the fundamental issues in the project;
- kept within their terms of reference except where information

103

elicited during the assignment clearly indicates that the terms need to be changed – and in the latter case have discussed with you any need for a change in the terms of reference with supporting evidence on why this is required;

- achieved the deliverables as set out in the project schedule, ie have met the deadlines and in general kept to the programme (subject to any agreed variations in the light of changed circumstances);
- kept within the agreed budgets for time and costs;
- provided clear and comprehensive progress reports as and when required;
- maintained good and informal contacts with you and your colleagues to discuss problems as they arise, test their understanding of the facts and review alternative diagnoses and solutions;
- been prepared to ask awkward and difficult questions and to probe, politely but firmly;
- developed good relationships with members of the organisation based on trust, effective communication and mutual support;
- been prepared to listen as well as to deliver pronouncements without adopting an arrogant approach which implies that they know all the answers;
- tested alternative recommendations with you and your colleagues.

Recommendations checklist

You should satisfy yourself that the consultants have produced recommendations which:

- meet the terms of reference (as modified if appropriate);
- follow logically from the analysis and diagnosis;
- are robust in the sense that they are practical and convincing, and address the real needs of the organisation;
- demonstrate that they have added value by making full use of their expertise and innovatory skills;
- take account of the culture of the organisation, its values, norms and management style;

- take account of the likely reactions of those affected;
- spell out the benefits and the costs;
- set out a practical programme for implementation indicating the steps to be taken, the timetable, the phasing in of recommendations, the problems to be overcome, the communications necessary, the resources required and the costs involved.

Fulfilling your part of the contract

Your obligations to the project can be summed up as follows:

- to provide leadership and guidance as necessary without unduly interfering in the day-to-day activities of the consultants;
- to prepare the ground for the consultants so that your colleagues, employees in general, individual employees who may be affected by the project and trade unions know what the project is about, how the consultants will be operating and the part they should play – eg providing information and being reasonably accessible;
- to provide facilities for the consultants in the shape of office space, communication systems and administrative support;
- to help them as necessary in arranging interviews and meetings.
- to provide help as required in collecting and analysing information;
- to anticipate and deal with problems arising during the assignment, such as failures to meet deadlines, lack of progress in developing acceptable and realistic recommendations and poor interpersonal relationships between consultants and members of the organisation;
- to ensure that steering committees and project teams carry out their roles properly;
- to involve staff in the project as appropriate to develop 'ownership';
- to conduct progress meetings in accordance with the project timetable and carry out a rigorous check on the achievement of deliverables as well as discussing any problems which have arisen or new developments which need to be taken into account;

- to review recommendations, analysing and evaluating alternatives and assessing the degree to which they meet the assignment's objectives and terms of reference, the ease or difficulty with which they can be implemented, the costs and benefits involved, and the likely reactions of colleagues, employees in general, individual employees and trade unions;
- to discuss recommendations with interested parties so that objections can be dealt with and modifications made as necessary;
- to prepare a plan for implementation, taking account of the consultants' proposals but modifying them as necessary;
- to obtain final agreement to the recommendations and implementation plan from all concerned;
- to communicate the results of the study to employees, indicating how they will be affected and setting out the implementation programme;
- to ensure that the recommendations are implemented as planned while paying particular attention to change-management imperatives.

Monitoring progress

One large firm advises its consultants always to keep the initiative; if they lose it, they should get it back as quickly as possible – it is *their* engagement. The point of this advice is that consultants must be allowed the scope – within their terms of reference – to conduct the assignment as they see fit. As long as they deliver the results you want and things do not go wrong, it is not for you to interfere with the processes they follow. You should in any case have agreed these processes before the engagement began.

But as project leader you have the right to know what is going on, how the assignment is progressing and what new problems or developments have been exposed or arisen during the course of the study. If you are the sponsor of the project only you can be held accountable for its success.

Progress should always be monitored formally by means of 'milestone' meetings. These should have been programmed when planning the assignment, and should cover the following:

- a report from the consultants on their findings and conclusions to date;
- a check of deliverables against the agreed schedule;
- a check of the time taken and costs incurred to date against budget;
- a discussion of any problems which have arisen and the steps required to deal with them;
- a discussion of any new developments and their impact, if any, on the terms of reference or assignment programme.

Progress should also be reviewed informally. The consultants should be encouraged to discuss their interim conclusions with you and any problems as they arise. You do not want to be breathing down their neck all the time, but it is often a good idea to hold a regular informal or semi-formal meeting. For large-scale assignments in which consultants are working full time it may be worthwhile holding these every week or once a fortnight.

Interventions

Although you should not interfere with the consultants you may have to intervene if things are going wrong. If a problem has arisen, you should not wait until the next progress meeting to discuss it. If you are aware of the fact that the programme is slipping you should immediately ask why. If a consultant has seriously upset one of your colleagues you should find out what has gone wrong and what needs to be done to put it right (the fault could lie with either or both of the parties). If a consultant seems to be underperforming, say so out at the time, but ensure that you have good evidence on which to base your intervention. And if new developments come to your notice which affect the project, explore their implications as soon as possible with the consultants.

Optimising recommendations

Producing the optimum results from an assignment depends not only on the quality of the consultants but also on your contribution and those of your colleagues. Consultants are there to add value but they cannot do so alone.

What might be termed a consensus approach, as illustrated in Figure 10.1, is desirable. Overriding the whole process is senior management involvement, which may diminish as the project develops, and the achievement of employee commitment and ownership through involvement and consultation, which increases progressively throughout the assignment. The approaches and tasks incorporate a variety of interactions with those concerned and the setting up of focus groups, workshops and task forces to gather information, make decisions and prepare and implement action plans. The processes include the identification of areas for change, involving decision making in developing and evaluating options and cultivating commitment to change. The programme is underpinned by process consulting which takes the form of collaboration, achieving consensus and iteration (rethinking initial solutions in the light of discussion and analysis).

Iteration may well be an important feature of this process of optimisation. Ideally you might expect the consultants to deliver a final solution which is instantly acceptable to everybody. But consultancy assignments, especially HR ones, are seldom like that. The consultants will indeed prepare recommendations but they may well identify alternative approaches (the 'one best way' seldom exists) which need to be evaluated. Achieving consensus may mean taking another look at both the initial and the alternative proposals on the basis of the views expressed by those involved in the consultation proceedings. And this process of iteration can continue until an optimum solution is obtained.

Clearly this does not apply to all assignments. There will often be a clear-cut recommendation to deal with a specific requirement or problem and that will be that. There are also obvious dangers in over-indulging in iteration. The outcome could be a bland solution which may partially satisfy everybody but does not address the real issues.

Planned implementation

The consultants may have full responsibility for producing practical recommendations, but the onus is on you to ensure in discussion with them that their proposals can be implemented

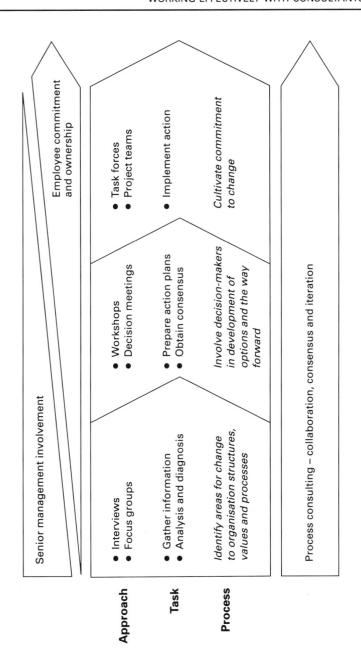

Figure 10.1 *The consensus approach to consulting*

without undue strain. You cannot wait until the final conclusions are reached. You must begin to assess the implications as soon as the first signs have emerged of how the project is likely to conclude.

Interim and final proposals and alternative courses of action need to be evaluated to assess the practicalities of implementation, the resources required and available, the costs involved and likely reactions. You cannot, however, allow yourself to be unduly swayed by the possibility of negative reactions from some quarters – this is inevitable in any assignment which leads to major changes in organisation, roles, systems and procedures or is likely to have detrimental effects on status, prospects or continued employment.

You should consider how any possible objections can be handled. Clearly, you must be reasonably certain that the ultimate decision makers will agree to implementation and that any powerful individuals or groups who could wreck the project can be persuaded to support it. This process of gaining commitment and ownership should not be left to the implementation stage. Progressively through the assignment you and the consultants should be testing reactions to any controversial aspects of the project and enlisting support for the likely conclusions.

Communication and consultation

The importance of good communication and consultation throughout an assignment cannot be overemphasised. You should expect the consultants to keep closely in touch with opinion formers and special interest groups, but you can help them to do this by encouraging interaction between them and anyone who is interested in or affected by the project. The more the consultants can communicate during the course of the assignment the less the likelihood of a shocked reaction to radical proposals.

The same principle applies to consultation and involvement. The motto of all HR consultants and HR managers who are carrying out a change agent role should be that people support what they help to create. The aim must be to ensure as far as possible that those affected by the project 'own' the solution and this can only be achieved if they are involved in developing it.

Approaches to implementation and change management are discussed in the next chapter.

Your role if you are not the sponsor

So far in this chapter I have assumed that you are the sponsor of the assignment, accountable for the results it achieves and ultimately responsible for its control. There may, however, be occasions when the project is sponsored by another party or group, such as the chief executive or non-executive directors. Such assignments may take the form of strategic reviews of the organisation, with implications for structures, HR strategies and policies, and the employment and career prospects of staff.

You may not have control over the assignment but you can through the consultants, influence its outcome. It is therefore desirable to ensure that you are involved and to build good relationships with them. If they are looking into any aspect of the organisation which has HR implications (and what aspect does not have) they should know that they will have your full co-operation in providing information and discussing the HR aspects of their findings. Consultants are often fully aware of the fact that the HR director has a wider knowledge of what is going on in the organisation than any other director. They need this sort of information and they will gladly come to you for it, which gives you an opportunity to make your contribution to their thinking.

111

11

Implementation

The outcome of a consultancy project should be an implementation plan. It is your job to ensure that the plan is realistic, cost-effective and achievable within a suitable time scale and that the required resources of people and money are available.

The implementation plan might involve major changes to structures, roles, processes, systems and procedures. It could involve a massive training programme or a number of recruitment projects, or movements of people into new or changed roles or down-sizing. The all-important transition from the present to the proposed arrangements will need to be controlled, and this may mean the careful scheduling and phasing in of the new structures or systems.

There will be situations when the new arrangements can be implemented immediately or when they *have* to be put into effect without delay to overcome a pressing problem. But an incremental approach will often be better, introducing the new arrangements one step at a time or progressively in different divisions or departments of the organisation. This gives people time to understand the implications, to become familiar with new roles or demands and to learn any additional skills they may need. It avoids loading too much change onto departments or individuals at once. After each stage you can pause to assess what has been achieved and any problems which have been encountered so that steps can be taken promptly to ensure that the next stage proceeds smoothly. It should be remembered that major culture change is always a long and often a difficult process. Do not expect too much to happen in the early stages.

The following is an example of how the stages of an implementation programme for the introduction of performance management might be defined. For each stage it would be necessary to indicate the timing and who will be responsible for managing the activities required.

1. Prepare briefing documentation.
2. Brief staff.
3. Prepare initial training programme, concentrating on setting objectives and concluding performance agreements but also covering in less detail the 'managing performance throughout the year' aspects of the process, ie interim performance reviews, revision of objectives and work plans and coaching and counselling techniques.
4. Conduct intial training programme.
5. Progressively, launch the initial performance agreement process.
6. Monitor the performance agreement process and take steps to remedy any defects.
7. Monitor the 'managing performance throughout the year' process and provide advice and help as required on any problems arising.
8. Plan follow-up training in conducting performance reviews and rating, and in coaching and counselling techniques.
9. Conduct follow-up training.
10. Progressively, launch performance-review process.
11. Monitor performance reviews and take steps to remedy any defects.
12. Evaluate the outcomes of the whole performance management process with the help of an attitude survey and plan any actions required in the shape of revised procedures, additional briefings or further training.

Help with implementation

You may decide that you can implement the plan yourself without outside help, and there is much to be said for this approach, not just because it will save money but, more importantly, because the implementation programme will be perceived as being owned by the organisation. It will thus display its confidence in its ability to manage the change. If you pursue this route you can convert a project team into a task force and give it the responsibility for the implementation programme.

Doing it yourself may be easiest and most appropriate when the changes to be implemented are within the normal operating boundaries of your department and can be seen as an extension of activities or services for which you are already responsible. It is more difficult when an extended programme of briefing, training, monitoring and follow-up is necessary. In these circumstances you may not have the resources required. You may also want to seek outside help with implementation if you feel that the knowledge and experience of the consultants who conducted the project is necessary for people to understand, accept and implement new processes or procedures.

Good process consultants in their change agent role can add value to any project by facilitating its implementation. Change management is a skill which all effective consultants know they have to master. Using outsiders to act as catalysts in the process can help to overcome resistance to change if they can show that they are acting objectively and can demonstrate by reference to their experiences elsewhere that their proposals will work and will be beneficial. They will also have the time to coach and counsel as necessary.

Managing change

If you start worrying about how to manage change at the implementation stage it is too late. At each of the earlier stages you should have been considering reactions and potential implementation problems and you should expect your consultants to be constantly aware of the need to build commitment to change progressively throughout the assignment.

At the outset, you should have communicated the objectives of the exercise to all concerned, both formally and informally. You should involve people as much as possible during the project in contributing to the diagnosis, discussing possible ways forward and testing interim recommendations. It is important to explore the implications for people in the organisation during these stages, to assess likely reactions and to take steps to handle any reservations or objections that may be raised. The constant aim should be to create ownership, and this can only be achieved by involvement.

When the final recommendations have been discussed and agreed it is necessary to brief everyone affected about what is going to happen. The briefing documentation should be as simple as possible – no jargon – and it should explain the benefits of the change for individuals as well as the organisation.

However, structural change and cost-cutting exercises are likely to have detrimental effects for some people, and a bland statement implying that what is good for the organisation will be good for them will, obviously, not be helpful. Individuals or groups who may be adversely affected should be briefed specifically, so that discussions can take place in advance on how the effects can be mitigated, perhaps by retraining, transfer, reducing numbers through natural wastage or voluntary redundancy or, as a last resort, outplacement advice.

The approach to change management

In a seminal article in the *Harvard Business Review*,[11] Michael Beer and his colleagues suggested that most change programmes are guided by a theory of change which is fundamentally flawed. This theory states that changes in attitudes lead to changes in behaviour. 'According to this model, change is like a conversion experience. Once people "get religion", changes in their behavior will surely follow.'

They believe that this theory gets the change process the wrong way round:

> In fact, individual behavior is powerfully shaped by the organizational roles people play. The most effective way to change behavior, therefore, is to put people into a new organizational context, which imposes new roles, responsibilities and relationships on them. This creates a situation that in a sense 'forces' new attitudes and behavior on people.

They prescribe six steps to effective change which concentrate on what they call 'task alignment' – reorganising employees' roles, responsibilities and relationships to solve specific business problems in small units where goals and tasks can be clearly defined. The aim of following the overlapping steps is to build a self-reinforcing cycle of commitment, co-ordination and competence. The steps are:

115

1. Mobilise commitment to change through the joint analysis of problems.
2. Develop a shared vision of how to organise and manage the achievement of goals such as competitiveness.
3. Foster consensus for the new vision, competence to enact it and cohesion to move it along.
4. Spread revitalisation to all departments without pushing it from the top – do not force the issue, let each department find its own way to the new organisation.
5. Institutionalise revitalisation through formal policies, systems and structures.
6. Monitor and adjust strategies in response to problems in the revitalisation process.

This approach is fundamental to the effective management of change. There are also a number of other guidelines, as set out below.

Guidelines for change management

- The achievement of sustainable change requires strong commitment and visionary leadership from the top.
- It is necessary to understand the culture of the organisation and the levers for change which are most likely to be effective in that culture.
- Those concerned with managing change at all levels should have the temperament and leadership skills appropriate to the circumstances of the organisation and its change strategies.
- It is important to build a working environment which is conducive to change. This means developing the firm as a learning organisation.
- Although there may be an overall strategy for change, it is best tackled incrementally (except in crisis conditions). The change programme should be broken down into actionable segments for which people can be held accountable.
- The reward system should encourage innovation and recognise success in achieving change.
- Change will always involve failure as well as success. The failures must be expected and learned from.

- Hard evidence and data on the need for change are the most powerful tools for its achievement, but establishing the need for change is easier than deciding how to satisfy it.
- It is easier to change behaviour by changing process, structure and systems than by changing attitudes or the corporate culture.
- There are always people in organisations who welcome the challenges and opportunities that change can provide. They are the ones to be chosen as change agents.
- Resistance to change is inevitable if the individuals concerned feel that they are going to be worse off, either implicitly or explicitly. The inept management of change will produce that reaction.
- In an age of global competition, technological innovation, turbulence, discontinuity, even chaos, change is inevitable and necessary. The organisation must do all it can to explain why change is essential and how it will affect everyone. Moreover, every effort must be made to protect the interests of those affected by change.

Gaining commitment to change

These guidelines point in one direction: having decided why changes are necessary, what the goals are and how they are to be achieved, the most important task is to gain the commitment of all concerned to the proposed change. A strategy for doing so should cover the following phases:

1. *Preparation*. The person or persons likely to be affected by the proposed change are made aware of the fact that a change is being contemplated.
2. *Acceptance*. Information is provided on the purpose of the change, how it is proposed to implement it and what effect it will have on those concerned. The aim is to achieve an understanding of what the change means and to obtain a positive reaction. This is more likely if:

   - the change is perceived to be consistent with the mission and values of the organisation;

- it is not thought to be threatening;
- it seems likely to meet the needs of those affected by it;
- there is a compelling and fully understood reason for it;
- those affected are involved in planning and implementing the change programme;
- it is understood that steps will be taken to mitigate any detrimental effects.

It may be difficult or even impossible to meet all these requirements, which is why the problems of gaining commitment to change should never be underestimated.

During this phase, the extent to which reactions are positive or negative can be noted and action taken accordingly. And it is at this stage that plans may have to be modified to cater for legitimate reservations or second thoughts.

3. *Commitment.* During the third phase, the change is implemented and becomes operational. The change process and people's reaction to it need to be monitored. There will inevitably be delays, setbacks, unforeseen problems and negative reactions from those faced with the reality of change. A response to these reactions is essential so that valid criticisms can be acted upon or explanations given of why it is believed that the change should proceed as planned.

Following implementation, the aim is to get the change adopted as, with use, its worth becomes evident. The decision is made at this stage whether to continue with the change or whether it needs to be modified or even aborted. Account should again be taken of the views of those involved.

Finally, and after further modifications as required, the change is institutionalised and becomes an inherent part of the organisation's culture and operations.

12
Using Internal
Consultants

More work is currently being outsourced to external consultants
who are eager to extend their basic remit of, for example, executive search, into broader areas such as management audits.
Within the organisation, however, HR professionals still have to
demonstrate that these consultants are providing added value
and that they can play a strategic role as business partners in the
management team.

These factors combine to emphasise the enabling role of the
HR department which exists, according to the Personnel Standards Lead Body, to 'contribute to the long-term success of the
organisation by forming and managing the environment in which
people's individual and collective contributions are max-
imised'.[12] It is no longer simply a service function, just there to
follow and support other people's ideas. At the highest levels it
has to provide leadership and innovation in all aspects of human
resource management and to help managers to learn and apply
new skills.

To achieve this new role the HR professional must be prepared
to intervene and exert some influence, using a contingency
approach – ie one which is tailored to meet the needs of the
situation. This can be done by functioning as an internal consultant, and increased attention is being given to this method of
operation. But the term 'internal consultancy' is often used
rather loosely and it is necessary to examine what it is, what
internal HR consultants or HR managers acting in a consultancy
mode actually do, the circumstances in which they may be
needed, the skills required and how they can best be used.

What is internal consultancy?

Internal consultancy is the provision from within the organisation of advice and services by conducting assignments which are

designed to develop and introduce new processes, systems and procedures or to provide solutions to management and operational problems. Internal consultants are therefore employees and their colleagues are their clients. It can be a full-time job with the designated title of consultant, in which case assignment fees for consultancy services are usually charged out. This is a typical arrangement in management services departments. It is less common in HR departments, however, although some local authorities such as Kent County Council and Southampton City Council are charging fees for personnel services and corporate personnel services are increasingly being provided on a fee-paying basis.

In one sense, any professional members of service departments such as IT, management accounting or personnel spend much of their time acting as consultants. They identify needs, respond to requests, carry out investigations, provide advice and help with implementation. These activities may not be on an assignment basis with defined terms of reference and agreed deliverables (although this is highly desirable) and the services may not be specifically charged for (although this is equally desirable), but they are using consultancy skills all the same. And such skills are becoming more and more crucial to the effective performance of an enabling role.

What do internal consultants do?

Internal consultants operate like their external counterparts, working alongside their clients to identify the need for new or improved approaches in the fields of policy, organisation, procedures and methods. They investigate problems, prepare proposals and help to implement agreed recommendations. But like all good consultants they are not there simply to solve other people's problems. Their aim is to build consensus and commitment to action and to facilitate learning so that their clients can operate independently and handle their own affairs without further guidance.

External consultants bring to their clients subject expertise, analytical and diagnostic skills, knowledge of other organisations, independence and objectivity. Internal consultants may have just as much expertise, although as employees it may be more difficult for them to be – or to be seen to be – as independent as those from outside the organisation. They have therefore to demonstrate that they are able to deliver truly objective advice.

Internal HR consultants can operate in three main areas:

- systems development – the introduction or amendment of systems such as those for reward, performance management and continuous development;
- service provision – the sort of recruitment, selection and training services that external consultants often provide;
- process consulting – advice and help in process areas such as organisation, team building, planning, objective setting, performance and reward management, quality management, conflict resolution and, importantly, change management. This is perhaps the most rewarding but also the most challenging field in which HR internal consultants can work: rewarding because they can be involved in the heart of the business, influencing the things that govern its success, challenging because it requires considerable skill and credibility, and because their lack of independence, as perceived by their clients, may work against them.

My own experience in the newly created post of Group Development and Training Manager at Rank Hovis McDougall illustrates what HR consultants do. There were at that time 80,000 people employed in literally hundreds of locations. The headquarters personnel function consisted of four professionals – we were ahead of our time. The only way in which I could operate was as an internal consultant, marketing my services, following up leads, identifying opportunities and selling the benefits of management development and training to divisional chief executives and unit general managers. My work was conducted entirely on an assignment or project basis: investigating high levels of staff turnover and developing improved selection and training schemes; recognising that the 'Cooks tour' type of induction training given to trainee general managers was ineffective and replacing it with a much shorter and more intensive project-based action-learning programme; or surveying the longer-term management needs of a division and working with the divisional chief executive to devise a career development system. In each case, the project was structured as a consultancy assignment, with terms of reference, statements of deliverables and the use of project management techniques to guide and monitor progress.

Other examples of internal consultancy projects which I have seen carried out by HR directors and their staff include:

- the introduction of performance management as a management process rather than yet another personnel system;
- the development of corporate planning processes in which line managers as well as the board participated;
- the facilitation of management conferences which involved managers in reviewing key issues and developing strategic plans;
- the co-ordination of the operation of a number of cross-functional project teams dealing with business problems and plans;
- the clarification of relationships between functions and areas of responsibility;
- the setting up of training and development programmes for managers to run within their own departments.

How do they do it?

In carrying out internal consultancy projects the most important thing to remember is that managers do not want ready-made products. They value access to expertise, help in problem solving, an independent point of view and support in managing change, but they reject pat solutions. Internal consultants must therefore endeavour to understand what managers want as well as what they need. As I have said, the art of consultancy is sometimes bringing wants and needs together.

Internal consultants should be well placed to identify needs as they arise. They do not have to wait to be asked, like external consultants. They should have a clear understanding of the strategic imperatives of the organisation, its business plans, the changing environment in which it has to operate, its culture and its dynamics. Their advice must be embedded in this understanding.

A typical internal consultancy project dealing with systems development will be conducted on exactly the same lines as an external project, ie it will consist of the following phases: contact, contract (deliverables and costs), data collection, analysis, diagnosis, feedback, discussion and agreement of recommendations, and implementation. A service-delivery project will also be similar; it will be a simpler affair of defining terms of reference, agreeing programmes and procedures, conducting the assignment and reviewing results.

Process consulting will be more complex and demanding. It is, as mentioned in Chapter 2, essentially a collaborative approach in which consultants are involved with their clients in gathering information, analysing and diagnosing needs and problems, and obtaining agreement to courses of action and commitment to change.

When are internal consultants needed?

In what circumstances do you need to have internal HR consultants, either on a permanent or on a seconded basis? In one sense, the answer is that any HR professionals who operate in an advisory capacity with managers on systems, processes and problem solving are acting in a consultancy role, whether or not they are actually called internal consultants.

It may, however, be appropriate to underline the consultancy nature of their work by calling them internal consultants, especially if they are exclusively concerned in project work rather than in providing continuing administrative or support services. And it would be even more appropriate if their services were being charged out to internal clients. This approach is being adopted increasingly, especially in the public sector in authorities such as New Forest District Council. The decision on whether or not to follow this route will depend on the amount of project work that is anticipated and also the culture of the organisation in the sense of how it wants to conduct its affairs. An argument sometimes used in favour of establishing internal consultants on a full-time basis is that this recognises the special nature of their role, gives them extra status and enables the organisation to identify people with the right skills and help in their further development.

Another approach is to second existing staff to internal consultancy projects. Again, in many cases this would be similar to what is already happening. A training specialist who is seconded to a joint project on the development of a new computerised system to advise on training implications and requirements is carrying out exactly what such specialists *should* be doing to assist in new developments. The only difference may be an increased emphasis on the need to treat the project in exactly the same way as an external consultancy assignment, with clearly defined terms of reference, deliverables, deadlines, project review procedures and cost budgets. This approach has the advantage of not committing staff to project work which may not materialise.

Whether or not there are designated full-time internal consultants or individuals inside the organisation who act in that capacity from time to time, decisions may well have to be made on whether or not external consultancy advice is also required. This could mean that the outside consultants would take full responsibility for the project without any internal involvement or, preferably and more commonly, they would work with internal consultants. In the latter case the external adviser can take the lead, or act as a facilitator, or take responsibility for certain parts of the project, or lend a helping hand generally. The following questions need to be answered when making the choice:

- Have we internal consultants (or people who can act in that capacity) with the necessary skills and expertise for this project and the time to devote to it?
- Are there advantages in using internal consultants who fit our culture, understand 'the way things are done around here' and are familiar with our existing technologies and processes?
- Would it be an advantage to have internal consultants available who will understand the problems which may be encountered during the project (including people problems) and will be able to play a hands-on part in the management of change required during implementation?
- Do we need an entirely independent point of view?
- Are we convinced that our managers will listen to our own people on this matter?

- Is there a prime requirement to gain the benefit of the experiences of other organisations which external consultants should be able to provide?
- Can we afford to use external consultants?
- What is the point of having internal consultants if we are not going to use them?
- If we do engage external consultants, what role, if any, will our internal consultants have?

What skills are you looking for?

One of the key matters to be considered when making decisions on the employment of internal consultants is the skills they need.

Consultancy skills

Like all management consultants, internal consultants need analytical ability, diagnostic and interactive skills and the ability to communicate clearly and persuasively.

They must be able to understand their internal clients' situation and problems and work with them in developing solutions. But at the same time, they must remain independent and be capable of taking a disinterested and objective point of view. Their job is not simply to act in a service role, satisfying the expressed needs of their clients. They must be able to add value, helping their clients to take a wider view and to look at different approaches to problem resolution. This may be more difficult for internal consultants who may not be perceived by managers as having the expertise, range of experience, knowledge of good practice in other organisations, and ability to remain detached which external consultants possess.

Counselling skills

Internal HR consultants can often act in a counselling role which, as suggested by the Institute of Personnel Management's *Statement on Counselling in the Workplace*,[13] involves the processes of recognition and understanding, empowering and resourcing. An internal consultant needs to be skilful at all these processes.

- *Recognition and understanding* – recognising the indicators of problems and issues. This focuses on understanding the other person's perspective and communicating that understanding. It concentrates on ensuring that both parties have the same understanding of the situation. This is the 'listening' aspect of an internal consultant's role.
- *Empowering* – enabling managers to recognise their own problem or situation and encouraging them to express it. This may involve, in Egan's phrase, 'changing the picture'.[14] This process starts by talking through an issue to help change the manager's perspective and indicate a solution to the problem. But this does not always happen and the internal consultant may have to use the tougher skills of challenging and confronting, sharing his or her different perceptions and providing a different framework. The initial 'listening' phase should have established an atmosphere of acceptance and openness which enables this tougher stage to take the process forward into action.
- *Resourcing* – advising on the resources (including people, systems and procedures) required to manage the problem and guiding managers on the best method of obtaining, developing and using these resources.

Facilitating skills

Internal consultants have to be good facilitators, helping other people to help themselves. They should assist managers to formulate action plans and provide guidance as necessary. But they may have to do more than that, pointing the way and suggesting new approaches or alternative solutions. And they may have to mobilise the expertise (their own or other people's) required to get things done. Ultimately, however, their aim will be to ensure 'ownership' of the new process or development and they can only do this by closely involving managers in the project.

The overriding requirement

Overriding all these skills is the need to be alert and responsive to expressed or implicit needs. If a business issue with HR implications arises at a board meeting (and many do), the HR director must react immediately with a positive contribution. The same principle applies at all levels in the HR function. Internal consultants have to be opportunists in the best sense of the word. They must be sensitive to key business and associated human resourcing issues so that they can speedily intervene or exert influence. They should also be innovative, proposing initiatives in the development of organisational processes such as performance and reward management which fit the strategic agenda of the organisation.

Using internal consultants

There should be no differences between the ways in which internal consultants and external consultants are used. Approaches identical to those spelled out in Chapters 9–11 should be adopted to set up, manage and control the project. It will, however, be important to spell out the roles of internal consultants, especially when external consultants are also taking part in the project. The internal consultants should certainly be involved in the initial discussions and should also take part in planning the implementation programme and in the management of change processes which will be required.

The effectiveness of internal consultants depends not only on their skills but also on their ability to manage and to participate in projects effectively. They will be able to make a much greater contribution if it is clear that they have the support and confidence of top management. Being an internal consultant can be a lonely and frustrating job, one in which incumbents are quite likely to quote Matthew 11:57 from time to time: 'A prophet is not without honour, save in his own country and in his own house.' Internal consultants need support as well as expertise. But if they have both, they can make an important contribution to the introduction of new HR processes and systems and to solving HR problems; and if they are fully employed they do not cost as much as outsiders.

Conclusions

Internal consultants should be well placed to identify needs as they arise – they do not have to wait to be asked. They should have a clear understanding of the strategic imperatives of the organisation, its business plans, the changing environment in which it has to operate, its culture and its dynamics. Their advice must be embedded in this understanding.

Internal consultancy is a role in which HR specialists can make a valuable contribution to the success of their organisation, but no one should underestimate the demanding nature of the task. They are, however, ideally placed to carry it out, as Don Young points out:

> After all, a personnel manager *ought* to be able to understand the business context and the opportunities and threats coming from it, as well as any of his or her colleagues. And if the personnel manager does not understand the fabric and the complexities of the organization, the medium through which the business is delivered, then who does?[15]

13

What Can Go Wrong and How to Get It Right

There should be little risk of things going badly wrong if you take the steps I have suggested in previous chapters. And although some assignments are more successful than others disasters in the HR field are few and far between.

But Murphy's Law applies just as much in consultancy assignments as in any other areas of activity – if anything can go wrong it will. So it is as well to be prepared for the problems which might arise so that they can be avoided, anticipated or dealt with promptly.

Typical problems

The following are the most common problems and their remedies.

Changing needs

Problem New information emerges during the assignment which means that the original terms of reference or programme are no longer relevant.

Remedy Monitor progress throughout the assignment so that if changes in the circumstances or need take place, swift action can be taken to modify terms of reference or programmes.

Hostility to the project

Problem Hostility from management, employees or trade unions builds up, even erupts, during the course of the assignment.

Remedy Again, you should try to anticipate likely areas of hostility at the beginning of the project and take steps to win people over. During the assignment you can keep in touch, both formally and informally, with reactions, and intervene to defuse any problems. If there is conflict then it is necessary to confront it immediately and do whatever you can to produce an integrated solution with the parties involved.

Failure to meet deadlines

Problem Deadlines are not being met for any of the following reasons:

- the time required was underestimated;
- the consultants spent too much time collecting and analysing data;
- they were diverted (or diverted themselves) into carrying out additional work;
- insufficient help was provided;
- unforeseen problems arose;
- insufficient control was exercised over achieving the project programme, either by the consultants or by you.

Remedy The starting point is an agreement setting out a realistic programme and deadlines, taking into account the resources available and assessments of the difficulties which may be encountered. It is essential then to monitor the programme through formal progress meetings and informal discussions. Agreed deliverables should be checked off and steps taken to anticipate future delays. If the programme has already slipped, time should not be wasted on recriminations. You have to agree on what has gone wrong and what needs to be done to put it right.

Costs over budget

Problem Costs have escalated, either because they were underestimated in the first place or because too much time has been spent on the project. Expenses can also sometimes seem unduly high.

Remedy   You can avoid this problem if you negotiate a fixed-price contract for agreed deliverables. If not, you should monitor time spent and therefore costs and, if necessary, question them before the costs escalate. You can insist that the consultants justify their bills with a full statement of the time taken. This can be checked against your own records.

As far as possible the levels of expenses that can be incurred under different headings, such as travel, subsistence, data processing, surveys and printing, should be agreed in the contract. This should include the type and standard of travel arrangements and the standard of hotels used. The contract should spell out that extraordinary expenses will only be reimbursed if they have been cleared with you in advance. It is quite reasonable for you to request copies of receipts.

Inadequate consultants

Problem   A consultant, or even the whole team of consultants, is not up to the job. For example:

- deadlines are not being met;
- deliverables are not being achieved;
- time is being spent on unproductive activities;
- the quality of the analysis or diagnosis is inadequate;
- recommendations are based on inadequate diagnoses or a misunderstanding of the situation and your needs;
- recommendations are unclear, pedestrian or reached down from the shelf, lacking creativity and failing to provide the expected innovatory thrust and added value;
- productive relationships with you and other members of the organisation have not been established and maintained.

Remedy   Clearly, you will try to avoid any of these problems by appointing the right consultants in the first place, taking care to interview those who will actually be involved in the assignment – but you may not always get it right. Selection processes for consultants, like those for anyone else, are not infallible.

As in any other situation when things are going wrong you must establish the reason and what can be done about it, rather than attaching blame. It could be that a consultant is inadequate in some way or it might be the outcome of events beyond his or her control. If you do think that the consultant is at fault you should initially discuss the problem with him or her and agree what should be done about it. Only if this fails to have any effect should you take it up with their manager or director if you are dealing with a firm.

If, having tried to solve the problem in this way, you believe the situation is irremediable, you can then as a last resort ask for the consultant to be replaced (if you are dealing with a firm). You should, of course, explain your reasons for making the request and spell out any circumstances which indicate that it is not the consultant's professional competence that is being impugned – it is not necessarily the fault of the consultant that he or she does not 'fit' the organisation, and it would be a pity to damage someone's career without proper cause.

If you feel strongly that the firm or the consultant is failing to deliver, you have the right to terminate the assignment within the terms of any contractual arrangement for termination. But it is a drastic step which could reflect on you if it appears that you have appointed the wrong consultant or failed to manage the overall project properly.

Conflict

Problem   Conflict can sometimes arise between consultants and members of their client's organisation, with consultants being accused of being arrogant, rude, unreceptive or unco-operative, amongst other things.

Such accusations may be made simply because people do not like what the consultant is finding out or seems likely to recommend. They may decide to defend themselves by going on the attack. Other people find it difficult to accept that if consultants are investigating a problem, they must probe and ask awkward questions. Their resentment at the exposure is projected onto the consultant. On the other hand, the consultant may actually *be* arrogant, rude etc.

Remedy   If such complaints arise you must try to establish whether the consultants were simply doing their job or whether they had overreached themselves. You have to consider whether people are being over-sensitive or whether, from the knowledge you have gained of how the consultants are operating or from other complaints, there is some substance to the allegations.

If you think there is some substance, then you should take it up with the consultants – a delicate and sometimes difficult job, but one that must be done. You cannot allow such complaints to fester. If, in your view, the complaints cannot be substantiated you may have to face the equally difficult task of persuading those who have made them that their accusations are groundless, perhaps pointing out in effect that the consultants are only doing their job. It is your duty to the project to back your consultants in such circumstances.

Conclusions

Some of these difficulties can arise in any assignment, but it is usually possible to take preventative or remedial action which removes, or at least alleviates, them. If they are based on interpersonal problems they can be hard to overcome but one of your tasks as sponsor is to create a climate of goodwill in the interests of achieving a successful outcome which will facilitate problem solving. In any case, you cannot expect consultancy assignments to go smoothly at all times. They may be dealing with fundamental issues about which people feel strongly and they may challenge assumptions, question past practices and current behaviour and present difficult choices for the future. Do not launch a major consultancy project unless you are prepared to manage the concerns that will inevitably result.

Case studies

The following brief case studies illustrate how some assignments can go wrong.

Installing a computerised personnel information system

This project took place in the early days of such systems. The company had installed some fairly sophisticated IT systems in

other areas such as customer order processing. The Personnel
Director obtained agreement from the board for the development
of a tailor-made stand-alone system. It was felt that the existing
packages would not fit the need and it was decided that the system would use personal computers networked with a minicom-
puter used mainly by the Operations Research Department.

A non-executive director (a powerful figure) strongly recommended a US-based firm which his company had used there and
which had recently started operating in the UK. The Personnel
Director took advantage of a business trip to America to meet the
Vice President, Marketing of the consultancy firm, who showed
him how they operated and arranged visits to installations in
New York and Detroit. The Personnel Director was impressed,
although he was only semi-literate in computers. He returned to
the UK, obtained agreement to go ahead with this firm and contacted the Vice President in America to arrange for the setting up
of the project. The Vice President came to the UK and a meeting
was arranged with the newly appointed Managing Director of the
UK consultancy operation. A programme and budget were
agreed and it was understood that the development would be
conducted in America.

A fairly young British IT consultant who had recently been
recruited was assigned to the project. He made a favourable initial impression and a miniature project team was set up reporting
to the Personnel Director and consisting of the Personnel Manager (something of a computer buff), a systems analyst from the
firm's computer department and the consultant.

At first all went well. The systems analysis was carried out
entirely by the consultant (the company's analyst being too busy
on other projects to make any real contribution). The Personnel
Manager agreed the systems specification, which was cleared
with the Personnel Director. The consultant then prepared the
detailed specification for the US parent company to design the
software. He was a few days late in doing this but the delay was
not significant.

After that, there was silence: nothing was heard from America
for weeks. Pressure was put on the consultant, the UK Managing
Director and the US Vice President; still nothing happened. The
software was delayed by a number of weeks and a fractious
meeting was held with the consultant (the UK Managing Direc-

tor being mysteriously absent), in which the speedy delivery of the software was insisted upon. Eventually it arrived, eight weeks late – and it did not work. It was checked by the firm's own IT Development Manager who stated unequivocally that it was an appalling piece of work and totally unacceptable.

The Personnel Director then called in the consultant and terminated the assignment. There was a howl of protest from the UK Managing Director and the US Vice President of the consultancy firm, who claimed there were only a few bugs in the system. But it was clear to both the Personnel Director and the Personnel Manager that the consultant did not really know what he was talking about, and had failed to carry out a proper systems analysis. The Personnel Director was adamant that the consultants had to be sacked.

An internal project team was then set up, headed by the Personnel Manager, and with expert and guaranteed help from the Computer Systems Development Department, a project schedule was drawn up. The system was produced on time – and it worked.

This débâcle cost the company several thousand pounds and in the post mortem the Personnel Director recognised, without being prompted, that he had made every mistake in the book. These included:

- relying on a recommendation without following up on how much the individual making the recommendation knew about the consultancy (it transpired that he knew little except that one of his colleagues in America had used the firm successfully on a finance systems project);
- not approaching any other firms to obtain alternative proposals;
- not taking up references;
- not seeing and approving the consultant before he was assigned (it was discovered that while he was an experienced business systems analyst, he had not dealt with personnel systems before);
- allowing the most important part of the assignment to be conducted outside the control of the project team, making it impossible to check progress or test the system at various stages in its development;

- not ensuring that the internal project team had sufficient IT resources available;
- failing to understand that this project could have been done internally – in other words, being mesmerised by the attraction of an outside firm of so-called 'experts' and ignoring the skills available within the company.

Introducing quality circles

With the help of consultants, this company had successfully introduced quality circles into its main plant. Using the same consultants, it now wanted to extend them into another of its plants in the north-east of England which had about 200 shopfloor workers, all of whom were trade union members (a different union from the one representing the other manual workers employed by the company).

There had been no problems with the first union but the Personnel Director was aware that the union representing workers in the north-eastern factory might have some objections to quality circles. He thought that the grounds for their objections would be that quality circles were a device for undermining the authority of the trade union, because they would by-pass the normal channels of consultation and negotiation which were very much union-orientated.

He discussed the project with the Chief Shop Steward and his deputy who, without being enthusiastic, had no objections. He went even further and had an informal word with both the District Officer and the National Officer for this section of the union, neither of whom expressed any concern.

The consultants were then engaged and a meeting was called of the full committee of union representatives so that they could be briefed by the consultants and agree on how they and their members might take part in the project.

Before this meeting, the Personnel Director was astonished to see the following notice which had been circulated to all the workers by a shop steward (not the Chief Shop Steward or his deputy):

QUALITY CIRCLES LOSE JOBS

The mention of Quality Circles should make any valid workers shake with fear at the thought of losing their jobs. Because this is what Quality Circles mean job stripping.

Nobody knows this better than the consultants used to introduce Quality Circles. When these consultants were called into the County Council with a view of introducing Quality Circles they charged an estimated £500,000. For this fee they job stripped over 2,000 jobs.

Other ways in which consultants work is to get the workforce to job strip themselves.

So if you belong to a team involved in Quality Circles BEWARE your best friend is not after your job.

There was, of course, no truth in the allegations about the consultants. They had indeed carried out an assignment for the local county council but it had nothing to do with quality circles, it did not cost £500,000 and it did not result in any immediate job losses at all.

But the damage had been done. At the meeting with the shop stewards a strong faction refused to co-operate in the introduction of quality circles in spite of the assurances of the Personnel Director and the consultant that the union would *not* be by-passed and that there would be no direct job losses. Perhaps they overdid it – at one point the Factory Manager whispered to the Personnel Director, 'You're protesting too much.' The project was abandoned.

The main lesson to be learned from this experience is that many people are deeply suspicious of consultants, whom they associate (not always without cause) with job-stripping exercises. The possibility of these fears emerging as major obstacles to progress, even when they are totally unfounded, has to be recognised. In this case an attempt was made to consult in advance, but it was not enough. It would have been far better to get the whole committee together at the outset and discuss with them the principles of quality circles and how *they* as well as the company would benefit. An agreement could then have been reached about the role of the consultants in helping to develop the system, suggesting that the facilitator, who would effectively control the quality-circle process, could be one of the union's

137

members. A similar approach had been used successfully when introducing a bonus scheme which involved training union members in work measurement techniques and involving them in checking standards.

A problem-solving course

The Chief Executive of this company believed strongly that his directors and managers were no good at problem solving. He therefore instructed the Personnel Manager to run an internal course for senior managers; he did not want them to be sent away on a course as he felt it was a waste of time and money and more value could be obtained by using company problems as case-study material.

The Personnel Manager obeyed these instructions and, with his Training Officer, selected a training consultant with experience in running such a course, having seen two other firms. The consultant was given plenty of time to meet people within the organisation to get a feel for the culture and the sort of problems managers dealt with. He also assembled case-study material.

The programme for a three-day residential course was then agreed with the Personnel Manager and 12 managers attended the first of what was intended to be a series. It failed. Participants made the usual remarks about the value of getting to know their colleagues better in the informal surroundings of a training centre, and said that on the whole they enjoyed the sessions and liked the consultant. But they could not understand why they had been sent on a course in the first place. One comment was: 'It was a complete waste of time; I wouldn't be where I am now if I couldn't make good decisions.' They could also not accept that a systematic, step-by-step problem-solving method was any use to them in the fluid, ever-changing environment in which they worked.

No blame could be attached to the consultant. He had done his best and his methodology could not be faulted. The failure was almost entirely attributable to the fact that the concept was flawed. It was a whim of the Chief Executive. Perhaps the Personnel Manager should have pressed strongly for a more systematic analysis of management training needs, which might have attached less priority to problem solving. Perhaps more effort should have been made to convince managers that ultimately they would benefit, but this too would probably not have succeeded. There was no clear perception of the need.

The main lesson from this experience is that you have to be absolutely certain that there is a real need for the project.

Getting it right

In each of the cases outlined above the problems were avoidable, and in each case it was up to the client to avoid them. The following lists summarise the main points to remember if you want to achieve results and add value through a consultancy project.

Do:

- take care to identify and define the real need or problem;
- decide on the results you want and define how these results will be measured;
- explore alternative ways of carrying out the project internally;
- determine the type of consultancy or consultant you want to meet your needs;
- consider more than one consultant;
- define specific terms of reference and deliverables;
- select consultants with relevant expertise and a good track record in the field who have demonstrated their ability to get results;
- select consultants on the basis of the added value they will provide, not their cost;
- select consultants who can offer continuity;
- select consultants who can show that they are making continuous efforts to update their knowledge and skills and keep abreast with new ideas;
- use referrals, if you have confidence in the information you are given – if not, use the IPM or MCIS registers;
- take up references with organisations where a similar assignment has been carried out by the consultant who is proposed for the project;
- agree a tightly defined budget;

- draw up a programme with progress review dates for the achievement of agreed deliverables;
- assign internal staff to the project to contribute their knowledge and ideas, learn from the consultants and carry out some of the information-gathering and analytical work, so cutting consultancy costs;
- keep all concerned within the organisation informed of the purpose and progress of the project;
- involve internal staff wherever possible in considering options, testing ideas and evaluating recommendations;
- monitor progress carefully against an agreed timetable and budget;
- be prepared to modify the terms of reference or the programme if new circumstances arise;
- evaluate all recommendations on the basis of the degree to which they meet objectives, the ease of implementation, their costs, the benefits arising from them and their acceptability to key decision makers and interest groups;
- draw up an implementation programme involving those affected wherever possible.

Do not:

- assume too readily that external consultants are the answer;
- rely on referrals – always check;
- allow consultants to be assigned to the project until you have checked their suitability from the point of view of their experience and expertise and the degree to which they will 'fit' the organisation;
- accept open-ended assignments as far as time and costs are concerned – always tie the consultants down to a budget and insist that no extra work is carried out unless they have obtained your prior agreement;
- allow the consultants to waste too much time collecting information which your own staff could easily supply;
- let the consultants carry on for too long without submitting progress reports;
- hesitate to intervene promptly and firmly if there seems any likelihood of serious slippage in the programme, of costs running above budget or of deviations from the terms of reference;

- allow the consultants to get away with half-baked recommendations or pre-packaged solutions – you have the right to expect that proposals are thought through and that a creative approach has been adopted.

Conclusions

There are more 'dos' than 'do nots'. Getting results and added value from consultants is a positive process. Of course, it is in the nature of things that consultancy projects will not always run smoothly. The problems may be almost intractable, internal politics may get in the way and circumstances and needs can change rapidly. But the systematic approach advocated in this book should ensure that difficulties can be overcome and a positive and beneficial result obtained.

Appendix A

Examples of Terms of Reference for Different Projects

HR strategies

- Review current and projected business strategies and assess their HR implications.
- Review current and projected HR strategies in the light of the business strategies.
- Conduct a broad review of the internal and external environmental factors affecting HR strategies.
- Recommend a framework for the development of HR strategies.
- Assist in the development of HR strategies within that framework.

HR policies

- Analyse existing policies in each of the main areas of human resource management.
- Conduct an attitude survey in order to establish the views of employees about existing policies.
- Identify in conjunction with management and selected groups of employees the current core values of the organisation and how they are applied.
- Provide information on the ways in which other organisations have expressed their HR policies.
- Facilitate a joint management/employee review of HR policies in the light of the data assembled as listed above.
- Provide help as required in drafting new or revised policies.

Procedure review

- Review existing procedures or practices against legal requirements.

- Obtain the views of management, employees and trade union or employee representatives about the effectiveness of the existing procedures.
- Prepare recommendations on any revisions required.
- Assist as required in consultations with trade union or employee representatives on the wording or rewording of procedures.
- Prepare notes for guidance on the administration of the procedures.
- Conduct briefing and training programmes on the operation of the procedures.

Problem solving

High levels of employee turnover

- Analyse turnover and retention rates for each major category of employee by location.
- Review the quality of job and person specifications to establish the extent to which they provide a reliable guide to the sort of people required and where they may be found.
- Assess sourcing procedures to establish the degree to which appropriate sources of recruits are being used.
- Assess recruitment and selection procedures. In particular, establish whether or not appropriate interviewing, testing and assessment techniques are being used and form views on the quality of the interviews carried out by members of the HR department and line managers.
- Review the effectiveness of induction training.
- Assess the degree to which levels of pay are competitive.
- Identify any other factors arising from the ways employees are treated which may contribute to high turnover/poor retention rates. These factors may include poor management or supervision, lack of challenge or opportunity, under-use of skills and abilities, unrealistic expectations of what employees can deliver, rewards unrelated to performance or contribution, unfair or discriminatory treatment or lack of continuation training.
- Identify any other considerations which may affect turnover such as insecurity, poor working conditions, unsocial hours or health and safety problems.

- Form conclusions about the main factors contributing to high turnover/poor retention rates.
- Make recommendations on the actions to be taken to overcome these negative factors.

Poor performance

- Establish key performance indicators and success criteria.
- Measure performance against these criteria.
- Identify the possible causes of poor performance. These may include poor leadership from managers or supervisors, inadequate equipment, bureaucratic procedures, bad selection or placement, lack of training, poor motivation or inadequate understanding or roles and performance requirements.
- Offer solutions to any problems that have been identified, such as management/supervisory training, skills training, performance-related pay or a performance-management system.
- Assist as required in the implementation of agreed recommendations.

Management succession

- Prepare supply forecasts of potential senior managers from within the organisation.
- Prepare demand forecasts of future requirements.
- Analyse competence requirements for senior management posts.
- Prepare an assessment centre programme.
- Train senior managers on their roles in an assessment centre.
- Organise and manage an assessment centre.
- Advise as required on further training and development programmes for those who have successfully completed the assessment centre.

Management audit

- Review the capabilities of existing senior managers.
- Assess potential for appointment to particular posts.
- Advise on any training or development activities required to improve performance and potential.

- Advise on any other action that may be required.

Industrial relations

- Conduct a survey of the current climate of industrial relations taking into account the views of line management, members of the HR function, trade union officials and representatives, and employee members of trade unions.
- Examine current procedure agreements in the light of this survey to identify any aspects which may need to be changed.
- Review the bargaining structure with particular reference to the scope for decentralised or single-table bargaining.
- Assess the case for recognising or derecognising trade unions and recommend appropriate courses of action.
- Review arrangements for involvement and joint consultation and make recommendations for improvement.
- Assess the various channels of communication and advise on any changes required.
- Review all other aspects of employment which might affect the climate of industrial relations and indicate any areas to which attention needs to be given.

Teamwork/interdepartmental conflict

- Identify through discussions with managers, supervisors and staff any areas where there is a lack of teamwork or where interdepartmental conflicts exist.
- Establish as far as possible the reasons for poor teamwork or conflict with the parties concerned, in particular the extent to which problems are caused by poor leadership, insufficiently clear definitions of roles and areas of authority, lack of understanding of the requirements for co-operation, rivalry (for whatever reason), power politics (for whatever reason) or overemphasis on individualism rather than teamwork (perhaps encouraged by an individual performance-related pay scheme).

Organisation

- Gain an understanding of the mission, strategies, main activities and culture (values, norms and management style) of the organisation.

- Identify the present and projected internal and external environmental factors which may affect the structure.
- Analyse the existing structure with particular reference to the allocation of authority for decision making, the allocation and grouping of responsibility for activities, the degree to which authority is centralised or decentralised and the hierarchies or layers that exist.
- Conduct an analysis of the strengths and weaknesses of the organisation against the background of the initial analysis of mission, strategies, objectives, culture and environmental factors. Pay particular attention to any symptoms of organisational weaknesses such as role ambiguity, poor teamwork, conflict, indecisiveness, an excessively bureaucratic approach, too much autocratic direction from the centre, lack of adequate control or co-ordination of decentralised activities, overmanning or duplication of activities.
- Diagnose the cause of any weaknesses, taking into account both structural and process factors. Under the heading of structural factors, attention should be paid to such features as inadequate definition of roles and authorities, the illogical grouping of activities, overlapping activities, to wide or too narrow spans of control, an overextended hierarchy (too many management layers), and overcentralisation or decentralisation. Under the heading of process factors, attention should be paid to any failure to integrate activities or to create high performance teams, too much interdepartmental rivalry and conflict, inadequate management, values or norms which do not support the effective organisation, co-ordination and integration of activities, and a lack of adequate systems support.
- Consider possible remedial action, taking account of both structural and process factors.
- Prepare and agree recommendations for restructuring or for dealing with process weaknesses.
- Assist as required in implementing agreed recommendations.

Human resource planning

- Analyse trends in the demand for and supply of people from within the organisation.
- Analyse external environmental factors which might affect the demand for or supply of human resources.
- Develop a planning model and provide training in its use.
- Carry out initial runs of the planning model in conjunction with members of the organisation and make any modifications as required.
- Advise as necessary on the implications of the output of these initial runs and the means of application available to the organisation.

Job evaluation

- Advise on the communication to employees of the purpose of the exercise and how it will be conducted.
- Advise on setting up a job evaluation panel and facilitate the operation of the panel.
- Provide guidance to the panel on the choice of a method of evaluation and the design of a factor plan, including the selection, definition and weighting of factors.
- Assist in the selection of benchmark jobs for analysis and evaluation.
- Train panel members in methods of job analysis and provide practical guidance to each panel member on his or her initial analysis.
- Review and comment on benchmark job analyses.
- Train panel members in job evaluation techniques.
- Guide panel members on the evaluation of the benchmark jobs.
- Discuss and agree with panel members any amendments required to the factor plan following the initial evaluation and, as necessary, take part in re-evaluating the benchmark jobs.
- Guide the panel in grading the benchmark jobs and designing of a grade structure.
- Advise and assist the panel as necessary in analysing, evaluating and grading the non-benchmark jobs.

- Provide recommendations on how the job-evaluation scheme should be administered and maintained.
- Advise on the way in which the grade structure and individual gradings should be communicated to employees.
- As required at the end of each stage of the assignment, report progress to a steering committee and discuss the outcome of the activities and deliberations of the panel.

Pay structure

- Select and analyse benchmark jobs for comparison purposes.
- Identify other organisations with which comparisons can be made and analyse relevant published surveys.
- Approach selected organisations to invite them to take part in the survey.
- Prepare capsule job descriptions of the benchmark jobs for comparison purposes.
- Ensure as far as possible that benchmark jobs are accurately matched with similar jobs in other organisations, by using a form of job evaluation if necessary.
- Collect and analyse the information provided by the comparator organisations and feed back summaries of the results to them.
- Analyse the information provided by published surveys on comparable jobs.
- Draw up a full comparison of internal and external rates, indicating where the company is positioned in relation to median and upper/lower quartile market rates.
- Draw conclusions about the competitive position of the company and discuss with management the company's pay policy or market stance, ie where it wants its pay levels to lie in relation to market rates.
- Advise on the implications of the market-rate data and pay-policy decision on the pay structure and make recommendations on the redesign of the structure as necessary.
- Provide advice as required on dealing with any anomalies in the pay structure.

Performance-related pay

- Advise on the organisation's objectives for performance-related pay.
- Analyse and review current arrangements for pay progression, performance appraisal and bonus payments.
- Hold discussions with managers, supervisors, employees and trade union representatives to establish the degree to which the organisation is ready for performance-related pay (giving particular attention to its culture, values and attitudes and the existence of suitable support from pay and appraisal systems).
- Develop preliminary recommendations for management on the type of performance-related pay scheme which is most likely to fit the culture and working environment of the organisation, and on the supporting performance review and rating schemes that will be required.
- Facilitate discussions with employees and trade union representatives on the purpose, design and operation of performance-related pay.
- In the light of these discussions, formulate recommendations on the design of the scheme, covering performance review and rating methods, the relationship between ratings and pay increases and rates of progression through pay ranges or zones, and methods of budgeting and controlling pay increases.
- Advise on methods of monitoring and evaluating the performance-related pay scheme.

Performance management

- Work with managers and employee representatives in defining the objectives of performance management and the approach the organisation wishes to use in operating it as a process of management and development involving all employees.
- Advise generally on the basic processes involved in performance management with particular reference to the formulation of performance agreements and work and personal development plans, approaches to managing performance throughout the year and methods of preparing for and conducting performance review meetings.

149

- Provide specific advice on methods of formulating and integrating corporate and individual work objectives at each level in the organisation.
- Assist in the development of generic competence definitions for key roles in the organisation.
- Make recommendations on the procedures and forms to be used in performance management.
- Prepare briefing documentation and notes for guidance, and assist in briefing as required.
- Prepare training programmes which cover setting objectives, agreeing competence requirements, formulating work and development plans, conducting review meetings, rating performance, and coaching and counselling techniques.
- Conduct and co-ordinate the training programmes in conjunction with members of the organisation.
- Advise on methods of monitoring and evaluating performance management with particular reference to the achievement of the maximum degree of consistency in performance ratings.

Appendix B
Addresses

Registers

IPM Consultancy Service
Institute of Personnel Management
IPM House
Camp Road
Wimbledon
London
SW19 4UX
Tel: 081-946 9100

Management Consultancy Information Service
38 Blenheim Avenue
Gants Hill
Ilford
Essex
IG2 6JQ
Tel: 081-554 4695

Listings

British Consultants' Bureau
Westminster Palace Gardens
1-7 Artillery Road
London
SW1P 7RJ
Tel: 071-222 3651

Directory of Management Consultants in the UK
TFPL Publishing
76 Park Road
London
NW1 4SH
Tel: 071-258 3740

The Personnel Manager's Yearbook
AP Information Services
Roman House
206 Golders Green Road
London
NW11 9PZ
Tel: 081-455 4550

Professional Institutions

Institute of Management Consultants
5th Floor
32-33 Hatton Gardens
London
EC1N 8DL
Tel: 071-242 2140

Management Consultancies Association
11 West Halkin Street
London
SW1X 8JL
Tel: 071-235 3897

References

1 PASCALE R. *Managing on the Edge*. London, Viking, 1990.
2 SCHMIDT W *and* JOHNSON A. *A Continuum of Consultancy Styles*, San Diego, University of Southern California, 1969.
3 TOWNSEND P. *Up the Organisation*, London, Michael Joseph, 1970.
4 GRAY D A. *Start and Run a Profitable Consulting Business*. London, Kogan Page, 1986.
5 *ibid.*
6 TURNER A. 'Consulting is more than giving advice'. *Harvard Business Review*, September-October 1982, p. 120–129.
7 *ibid.*
8 ING B. 'Customer first'. *Quality Briefing Note No. 5*. Institute of Management Consultants, London, 1993.
9 TURNER, *op cit.*
10 GRAY. *op cit.*
11 BEER M. *et al.* 'Why change programs don't produce change'. *Harvard Business Review*, November-December 1990, pp. 158–66.
12 PERSONNEL STANDARDS LEAD BODY, *A Perspective in Personnel*. London, PSLB, 1993.
13 INSTITUTE OF PERSONNEL MANAGEMENT. *Statement on Counselling in the Workplace*. London, IPM, 1992.
14 EGAN G. *The Skilled Helper: A systematic approach to effective helping*. London, Brooks Cole, 1990.
15 YOUNG D. 'Change and the personnel manager'. *The Human Resource Management Yearbook 1992*. London, AP Information Services.

Index

DEVELOPING SKILLS

Other titles in this series

Assessment Centres
Second edition
Charles Woodruffe

This acclaimed book explains how assessment centres can be a crucial tool for selection and development.
Charles Woodruffe examines:

- design and delivery
- personnel and participants
- feedback
- training techniques
- validation techniques

This revised second edition includes far more detailed consideration of development centres, the latest thinking on critical competencies, and likely future issues.

0 85292 545 X

Training Needs
Analysis and Evaluation
Frances and Roland Bee

Roland and Frances Bee argue that training needs must be driven from business needs and a corporate strategy developed in response to external and internal stimuli.

Once the need has been clearly specified, all the more technical issues fall easily into place.

Using many examples, this clear and practical guide describes a systematic four-stage evaluation process which allows managers to assess whether training has been successfully transferred to the workplace, whether it serves organisational objectives and provides value for money.

0 85292 547 6

Top Class Management
Lessons for Effectiveness
Edwin Singer and Richard Graham

Effective training builds on managers' need to acquire – and practise – a wide range of new skills. This superb book provides a compact portfolio of all the essential elements.

Drawing extensively on the authors' highly successful courses for British Rail and a leading rubber company, as well as many incisive examples from retailing, manufacturing, transportation and the public sector, it explains the nature of business, the market economy and management professionalism. Later chapters set out the basic philosophy and principles of:

- learning by doing
- making things happen – through people
- do-it-yourself strategic planning
- listening to the market and caring for customers
- harnessing data and measuring results
- working with groups and leading from the front
- reviewing and improving your performance
- becoming a better manager.

For anyone involved in developing managers or establishing a learning organisation – and all managers keen to get ahead – Graham and Singer offer both plentiful practical guidance and a unique stimulus to success.

0 85292 530 1

Interviews: Skills and strategy
John Courtis

This incisive book shows how a well prepared strategy and the right searching questions can lead to far more effective and quicker interviews. All the vital skills are included:

- attracting better candidates
- filtering out no-hopers
- selling the company
- spotting potential
- techniques for appraisal and counselling interviews
- support from testing and scored bio-data

0 85292 406 2

Everyone Needs a Mentor
How to foster talent within the organisation
Second edition
David Clutterbuck

Mentoring, once predominantly a North American phenomenon, has taken root in the UK and Europe. David Clutterbuck's popular book draws on the practical experience of British and European companies to illustrate best practice. The experience of these companies shows that mentoring is a valuable, rapid and cost-effective method of developing junior managers, recent graduates and minorities.

The book looks at how mentoring works, the benefits to the company, to the mentor and to the protege, and how to avoid some of the problems inherent within the organisation.

'This is a splendid little book for all those who want to know what mentoring is and how the process can help people to develop at work.'
Transition

0 85292 461·5

Job Analysis
A practical guide for managers
Second edition
Michael Pearn and Rajvinder Kandola

Job analysis offers a series of invaluable techniques for assessing how work is done – and how it could be done better.

Whenever managers try to define excellence or draw up job descriptions, identify career paths or evaluate a training scheme, job, task and role analysis count as vital tools. In this well-established text, two leading occupational psychologists examine the most effective modern methods and illustrate their use with fascinating real-life examples. Their extensively revised second edition includes full discussion of recent developments like the Work Profiling System and the competency framework. For all personnel specialists and many other managers, it offers a superb introduction to a crucial (but often neglected) area of expertise.

'This is essentially a practical text that focuses on an area which is of crucial importance to a manager and demonstrates how much more there is to 'job analysis' than time and motion study. It is brief, clear and to the point.'
Modern Management

0 85292 542 5

Outdoor Training for Employee Effectiveness
Mark Tuson

Drawing on extensive experience in the area of outdoor training, Mark Tuson shows in-house trainers, personnel specialists and senior managers how to:

- analyse needs and define objectives
- design (or commission) comfortable but stretching sets of tasks
- create physical and mental safety nets
- cope with hidden agendas, gender and cultural issues
- make the best use of focussed reviews
- transfer new skills and behaviours back to the workplace

0 85292 549 2

Effective Change
Twenty ways to make it happen
Andrew Leigh

Today's managers live in times of turbulent change. They can ignore change, resist it – or use it to improve their organisation.

Andrew Leigh has distilled the wisdom of the experts and created an invaluable toolkit of strategies, procedures and techniques for achieving effective change. His twenty ways include:

- team building
- commitment
- experimenting
- participative decision making
- tracking
- force field analysis
- verbal skills.

0 85292 412 7

Turning People On
The motivation challenge
Andrew Sargent

How does the manager gain the positive commitment of the workforce? What measures are necessary to motivate employees and make them effective members of the organisation?

Andrew Sargent explains the issues, the theories expounded by behavioural scientists, the barriers to motivation, the crucial influence of the personnel expert and, through description of actual case studies, the role of supervisors. He offers positive, practical and informative guidance to achieving harmonisation and motivating the team.

Above all, the book focuses on constructive analysis of the challenge of motivation and practical help in making it happen.

0 85292 444 5

Raising the Profile
Marketing the HR Function
David Clutterbuck and Desmond Dearlove

HR departments *know* they provide a vital service to their internal customers – so why do they often enjoy only grudging **respect?**

Largely, suggest David Clutterbuck and Desmond Dearlove in this stimulating handbook, because they neglect basic *marketing* skills. By segmenting their 'client base', developing the 'key accounts', soliciting and responding to feedback, creating an HR brand and constantly communicating the key messages, personnel practitioners can soon transform the way they are perceived. A commitment to quality and customer care is no optional extra, but clear evidence of HR professionalism; this invaluable book explains the essential techniques involved.

0 85292 526 3

For further information on the full range of IPM titles
please contact

The Publications Department
The Institute of Personnel Management
IPM House
Camp Road
London SW19 4UX
Tel: (081) 946 9100

CONSULTANCY
SERVICE

IPM Consultancy Service

An expert resource at your command

The variety of assignments in the field of human resources is immense. Different tasks require different skills and it is rare that any organisation possesses all the necessary skills at all times. The facility to call up specialist expertise in rapid response to a sudden requirement is, therefore, essential.

The IPM Consultancy Service provides you with experienced professionals to match your needs. It is the only service to carry the imprimatur of the professional body, the Institute of Personnel Management. The service is both pro-active and flexible, with IPM Consultancy Service monitoring the assignment and ensuring quality control on your behalf.

Support is available, throughout the UK on either a short or long term basis and each of our consultants is a recognised specialist in one or more areas of human resources. We are able to match industry experience and assignment expertise to ensure that the resource supplied – whether a large consultancy group or an independent – is familiar with your sector of business or industry as well as your particular requirement.

To get the specialists working for you

Simply call 081-946 9100 and give a description of your requirement. There is not a single human resources assignment which cannot be handled. We arrange a consultative meeting for a full briefing before producing written proposals with all costs. It could not be simpler.